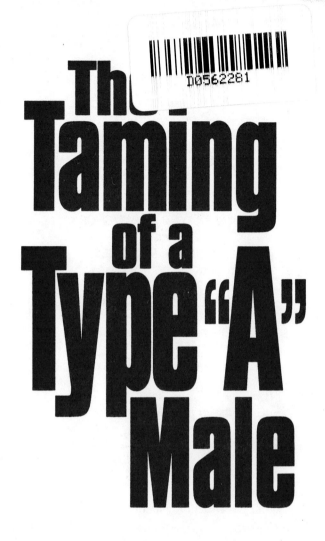

The Taming of a Type "A" Male

THE TAMING OF A TYPE A MALE
How to Gain Control by Losing It

formerly published as:
I PRAYED for PATIENCE
and other
HORROR STORIES

© 1989 by Chuck Snyder
Published by Questar Publishers, Inc.

Portions of this book are adapted from
OTHER THAN THAT, I HAVE NO OPINION
© 1983 by Chuck Snyder,
and published by Tyndale House Publishers, Inc.

PRINTED IN THE UNITED STATES OF AMERICA

ISBN 0-88070-571-X

For information:
QUESTAR PUBLISHERS, INC.
P.O. BOX 1720
SISTERS, OREGON 97759

93 94 95 96 97 98 99 00 01 -- 10 9 8 7 6 5 4 3 2

CHUCK SNYDER

The Taming of a Type "A" Male

How to Gain Control by Losin' It

MULTNOMAH

Sisters, Oregon 97759

Scripture references in this book are from
The Living Bible. My special thanks to the author,
Ken Taylor, for helping to change my life
and for allowing me to quote from
The Living Bible in this book.

To my sweetheart, Barb

I'm convinced I wouldn't be half the person
I am without her patience and enduring love.
She taught me how to communicate,
how to honor people, how to value
relationships. Thank you, dear Barb.
I will be eternally grateful.

CONTENTS

THIS BOOK
MAY BE HAZARDOUS

IF YOU LIVE IN THE REAL WORLD, I hope you'll take a journey with me through this book. I want to talk about my failures in a variety of everyday situations.

There was a time when the last thing I'd do would be to share my failures and weaknesses with you. But I've found a whole world of people out there who have the same struggles I do at times—yet we go through life with "How Are You?/I'm Fine" exchanges—when our marriages are near divorce, our kids are on drugs, we're afraid of failing in our jobs, and we can't get near God no matter how often we go to church. I've found that when I'm real and vulnerable, it helps other people be the same way, and we can share our lives as we learn the lessons God wants us to learn.

I have a "Type A" personality that gets me into all kinds of trouble. If you're not familiar with that term, it basically means that people with my personality hate bank lines, red lights, and waiting of any kind. We are "driven" to make every minute of every day count for something. The only thing we want is control of everything in our life including people, work, play, and even God at times.

Whether you are a Type A personality or not, I hope that you'll relate to some of the struggles I have gone through and will learn how important it is to go THROUGH them instead of trying to get OUT of them. But most importantly, I hope that by reading this book you will learn how to gain control of your life—by losing it. Sounds contradictory, doesn't it? But I believe after you hear my story, it will make sense.

I base my thoughts on principles from the Bible, and make no apologies for it. I've found that God is not some big, unreachable, untouchable, unreal force. He's a living Person who wants to influence my every waking moment, and to give meaning and purpose to my life. He's turning me around in so many areas of my life—although it's a continuing process, and I haven't arrived. But since the bottom line of Christianity is God's UNconditional love, I know He hasn't given up on me, and never will.

Even if you aren't into the Bible, I hope you won't put off reading this book because you think it will have a lot of religious jargon you won't understand, or will bore you to tears. I've tried to eliminate that type of thing. Just breeze on through anything you don't understand or agree with.

Actually, this isn't intended to be a "religious" book. Religion is stuffy and pious and self-righteous, and I don't want you to think of me that way. I hope you'll laugh, and maybe cry with me, as I tell my story.

Most of all, I hope you'll enjoy this book, whether or not you agree with what I've come to believe.

I want to warn you, however: *This book may be hazardous to some of your long-standing beliefs, opinions, feelings, prejudices, leanings, evaluations, impressions, estimations, or hunches.* Please read all of it before tar-and-feathering the author!

Thank you.

CHUCK SNYDER

PART I

HIGH-RISK LIVING

1

PORTRAITS
OF IMPATIENCE

WE CONTROLLERS HAVE TROUBLE with patience. Plan "A" never works out like we want it to. People will never do things right, or on our time schedule, or how WE would do it. And we get OUT of control. For example—

PATIENCE ON THE FREEWAY

When someone cuts me off on the freeway, my calm, reasoned, thoughtful, logical, justifiable approach is...TAIL-GATE THEM! BLINK MY LIGHTS! HONK MY HORN! SHAKE MY FIST! I also visualize the other car crashing in flames down a thousand-foot bank.

I know you're shocked, because you have never had feelings like that...but now you know one person in the world who does.

It even messes up my spiritual life. I pray a lot in the car, and sometimes the Lord and I are having a great old time of fellowship when some jerk pulls in front of me and I'll lose it. I then suggest to God that we talk later, because I don't feel all that spiritual.

I guess this is one reason I don't have bumper stickers on my car that say, "Isn't It Wonderful to Be a Christian" or "This Car Leaves the Road at the Rapture." I don't want God's reputation on the line every time I blow it on the road.

I take that back — I did try a small little dove on my bumper one time. Not many people would know what it meant, and those that did would be encouraged by my love for the Lord. When I mentioned the dove to one of my friends (who knows me quite well) he asked if I put it on the inside of the bumper. Nope. It was right out there for everyone to see, until the day a jerko in a big white van (I hate vans) came barreling up behind me on a single-lane road, and sat on my tail so close he would have touched me if my bumper had one more coat of chrome.

I had two options in responding to that situation:

(1) Pull over at the first opportunity, and let him go by, allowing the words of my mouth and the meditation of my heart to say something like, "Bless you, my son"; or,

(2) FIGHT BACK!

As it happened, I suddenly got a cramp in my accelerator foot, which caused my car to come to a crawl. You should have seen that fathead SQUIRM! He was ready to have a heart attack. The smile on my face was plain sin, but that just proves the Bible is right when it says sin is pleasurable for the moment.

Finally we got to a two-lane road where I could impede his progress no longer, and he was out of my life.

All of a sudden, I remembered the dove that had been shining right there in front of him. Hopefully, he just thought the dove indicated I was for "peace." But on the slim chance he really knew what it meant, he probably was saying to himself, "Those lousy Christians!"

When I got home I took off the dove, so I'm doveless again. Someday after the Lord works on my patience for a few more years, I might try a small fish or something. For the time being, I don't want the Lord's name associated with my mistakes on the highways and byways of our nation.

SOLUTION:

Drive only on roads with four lanes.

PATIENCE ON THE FREEWAY — Part Two

What happens if I'm the tailgater and the person in front of ME is going two miles per hour?

This situation occurs mostly when we decide to travel over the mountains to see Barb's mother. Barb loves to take the route that goes over Steven's Pass. She thinks it looks like the Swiss Alps. The scenery *is* spectacular, but the road is narrow and we regularly get behind 17 buses, 34 eighteen-wheelers loaded with either cement or steel beams, 67 RV's, 83 double-wide trailer houses, and 456 cars — of which 23 are driven by people over 100 years of age who drive so slowly because they have far fewer goals left to accomplish in life than I do. My job is to get around every single one of those vehicles before the trip is over.

There is only one logical reason why you would go over a mountain pass anyway, and that is to get wherever you are going. The second logical thing is to forget Steven's Pass, and head for Snoqualmie Pass, where you have four beautiful lanes and you can get around everyone and not spend your sunset years looking at the back of a logging truck.

Barb kept saying I made her life miserable whenever we went over Steven's Pass, so after I began learning the biblical principle of honoring her, I made a decision to change my attitude the next time we took the trip. We would go her way, and I would be patient, look at the scenery, stop for coffee, inspect all the restrooms, and maintain a spirit of happiness for the entire two weeks it took to travel the 130 miles.

The problem is, when I'm in the car I tend to go on automatic. (For example, when I'm on the way to church I sometimes find myself on the freeway headed for work.) So tragedy struck again the next time we went to her mother's. I automatically headed for Snoqualmie Pass, not Steven's, despite my honest intentions. I tried to turn around, but Barb would not hear of it.

A year or so later we did make it through Steven's Pass, and had a wonderful month going the 130 miles. We stayed at some beautiful hotels along the way. Just call me Mr. Patient.

SOLUTION:

Don't go over the mountains.
Write her mom a letter.

PATIENCE WITH MY DIET

I have started 327 diet plans that involved drinking 1,895 protein shakes, eating 7,653 fiber-filled "chocolate" bars that had about as much flavor as dental floss, and enduring hours that added up to days that added up to years of agony passing up those eclairs and extra helpings of potatoes and gravy.

One of the problems is that the world's vocabulary has changed. When I was a kid we had "juicy" bacon and "juicy" steaks. Now it's called "fat" or "greasy."

My cholesterol numbers are up too. Personally, I think it's hereditary. My dad, who is 85 at this writing, doesn't have cholesterol, but I'm sure some great-great-great-uncle who came over on the *Mayflower* had a horrible problem with the stuff.

I'm eating bran muffins for breakfast, if you can imagine

such a thing. And all they have in them is bran! I've asked Barb to add in chocolate chips, sugar, shortening and butter to make them more like the ones I get in the bakery, but I guess she likes to see me suffer. I wash down the muffins with Barley Green. (Don't laugh — there really is such a thing. It's the dried juice of barley plants.)

I'm sure it's all in my mind, but I don't seem to have the problem with allergies I used to have. It can't be from my eating habits, I'm sure. And by the way, the term "eating habits" is a sham. This phrase was invented by a skinny, oat-meal-loving fruitaholic who wanted to inflict his standards on the rest of the world. I realize I am supposed to lose weight, but not by changing my EATING HABITS, for good-ness' sake. The idea is to lose the weight so you can ENJOY your eating habits.

One of my biggest problems is that I have the world's biggest sweet tooth. I innocently stroll down the candy aisle at the supermarket or drug store and see 150 different kinds of chocolate bars staring me in the face, plus M & M's, banana treats, licorice sticks, and those "Easter eggs" that are pure sugar. (Excuse me, I have to go the store for a minute.)

(*Pause.*)

I'm back. Where was I?...Oh, that's right, the candy aisle. As I stroll through the chocolate forest I hear tiny voices call-ing, "Chhhuuuuuuuccckkkk..." You may not have known chocolate bars talk, but they do.

At this point I have to be very careful not to get too close to their cages, because they JUMP into my shopping cart and it's impossible to get them out once they are in. Once in a while I succeed.

Rocky Road candy bars are one of my very favorites, and one day I marched right down the candy aisle and looked those bars right in the label and didn't blink. I stood my ground, gritted my teeth, and went right on by...smack dab into the peanut clusters. Now there's no way even God would expect me to withstand peanut clusters after such a stirring victory over Rocky Roads, is there? I knew you would agree. So at $42.38 a pound, I buy some peanut clusters and walk out with a spring in my step, knowing I have stood STEELY FIRM against the Rocky Roads.

I eat a few peanut clusters, and then hide the remains under the front seat of the car. At some point right after lunch I feel so guilty I go get them and throw them into the garbage can. Timing is important on this, however, because my victory has to come on Thursday just before Friday, which is garbage day. If there is more than a day between throwaway day and garbage day, I have been known to "rescue" the peanut cluster remains, resulting in another bout of guilt.

I know you can't relate to all this, but at least you'll know how to pray for me better.

SOLUTION:

Stay out of the candy aisle.

PATIENCE WITH EXERCISE

One of my life verses is where the apostle Paul told us,

> Don't waste time arguing over foolish ideas and silly myths and legends. Spend your time and energy in the exercise of keeping spiritually fit. Bodily exercise is all right, but spiritual exercise is much more important and a tonic for all you do. (1 Timothy 4:8)

I take this to mean that we are not meant to run. I HATE to run, but sometimes I give in to some misguided reading I've done that says running is good for me. The confusing thing is that other people say if we run we'll get shin splints, or we'll pound our joints out of whack, or our little toes will fall off. These people probably just don't like to run.

Of course, NOBODY likes to run, except those few human beings who have passed the six-mile mark. There's something mysterious about the six-mile barrier. Once you have run six miles in one stretch, there's an audible snap in your brain and you LIKE to run. Some people have been known to run twenty-six miles at once. Somewhere in Boston, I think.

There are many benefits to running for people my age. They escape me just now, but I'll let you know when I think of them.

I should run, and someday I will. The problem is, I bleed for the first twenty minutes after I get out of my warm bed. I am what is known as (for want of a better term) a "progressive" sleeper. I set three alarm clocks: the clock radio, a battery one on the floor by my bed, and one on the dresser so I have to get up to turn it off. The idea is, when the first alarm goes off I can stir, but I know I really don't have to get up because the second alarm (set a half-hour later) will do the job. Then in six seconds (it seems) the second alarm goes off. I grab number two and three, and head for the middle bedroom where I doze a little more until the third one sounds the alarm for the day.

For some reason, Barb doesn't like three alarms going off. I don't know why she doesn't appreciate my efforts to get up and brave the world for her every day. She has been known to bolt straight up in bed on clock number one, and not be able to get back to sleep worrying about numbers two and three.

The reason I am trying to get up is to do my exercises and look like Mr. America. I've been trying to get new muscles since I turned thirty-five, but the atom-testing has caused my midsection to expand. Someone must have been messing with the balance of nature, because I don't eat any differently now than I did at twenty.

I can't do anything about exploding atoms, so I decided to get up and begin exercising. When I do something I like to do it right, so I resolve (usually right after dinner on New Year's Day, after the football games are over) each day to do one hundred push-ups, fifty chin-ups, and seventy-five sit-ups, to run ten miles, and to not have any candy or pizza for the rest of my life. I faithfully carry out my vow for two to three days, and when I don't look like Mr. America I decide to forget the whole thing. Why would I want to go through all that abuse if it doesn't make any difference?

Barb has this ridiculous idea of starting off by doing one push-up, two sit-ups, three chin-ups and running three blocks, and to work up from there, but what does she know about the manly art of exercising?

SOLUTION:

Don't weigh.

PATIENCE WITH WEDDINGS

I probably could make it through this life fairly well if I didn't go to one more wedding, but there are tons of people we want to honor, so I keep going. It's not that I don't love the kids involved. I really do. It's just that weddings try my patience because they are so inefficient.

First of all, they usually take place on Saturday afternoon during the NFL playoffs or World Series or some other important, world-changing event. I spend the morning dreading getting all dressed up, and of course the afternoon is shot, and part of the evening too, unless you can duck the reception.

The bride and groom don't know if we're there or not anyway. They just have eyes for each other. We may as well just sign the register book and then leave, and later the couple can read over the names and say, "Oh, look at that, Chuck and Barb were at our wedding." That would make it much simpler.

When we arrive at the church our intelligence is questioned because they don't think we can find our own seats. So we have to wait in a four-block line while two tuxedoed yuppie-types casually escort each lady down the aisle with her smiling husband who is screaming inside about missing a golf match.

After we get seated it finally dawns on someone that the candles aren't lit, so we have a couple of gals fire up the propane torches and light them one by one by one. It would seem like someone would catch that in rehearsal, because that would save a good twenty minutes right there.

For some reason the mothers didn't choose to be seated while everyone else was, so that has to be done next, costing more time.

Then someone sings fifteen verses of a song no one has ever heard before.

Then the wedding party enters. You can tell the difference in sexes right away. The guys usually just come in a group through a door near the front of the sanctuary, and they stand and wait (just like they'll be doing the rest of their lives). But do you think the girls can come in as a group? Not on your life. They have to plod down the aisle one by one, to the tune of Bach's funeral chant or something similar that drones on and on.

Once everyone has finally made it down the aisle, the pastor mumbles something to the couple, and then preaches a sermon for thirty minutes, knowing he won't have another chance at the folks until Easter.

At the end, it takes as long for everyone to get out as it did to get in, though it would be so much better if someone just said "Dismissed!" You could rush to the reception line and say how wonderful it all was, grab one of the dinky pieces of cake, and get out of there. But Barb wants to visit, so I stand around in my good clothes trying to keep the glaze out of my eyes.

SOLUTION:

Offer to drive a getaway car
so the couple can elope.

PATIENCE WITH SALESMEN

I'm a soft touch. I buy four boxes of Girl Scout cookies. I tip the kid at the parking lot even if I park my own car. When I find spiders, I gently lift them onto an envelope and escort them outside. And at the state fair I'm a sucker for those fast-talkers under umbrellas who sell salad-makers, kazoos, tattoos, blown glass, and knives that will never dull.

Once when we visited the state fair as newlyweds, we saw a guy showing off his blender. We were amazed. It chewed up ice, rocks, whole potatoes, and a screwdriver. The guy's watch fell in, and POOF, it was vaporized. There was nothing the blender wouldn't chew up as it combined lots of good things to make delicious milkshakes to keep our nutrition up. We decided we could no longer face our friends without a blender, so we purchased one.

Thinking back, I'm sure the man was honest, because at no time did he actually say OUR blender would do the same things his blender did. He was simply demonstrating what a blender could do if you have a ten-horse motor under the table. He just HAPPENED to have a stack of blenders on the table that resembled his, just in case any of us would like a blender that LOOKED like his blender. He was perfectly innocent.

On the way home, I had all these visions of growing strong with all the delicious drinks our new blender would make. In fact, I wanted to stop at a men's store on the way home and get a new wardrobe for my new muscles, but Barb thought we should get home.

I unpacked the blender, put in the ice, the whole potatoes, the screwdriver, my watch, and the artichoke hearts that were going to make me strong, and pushed the button. It groaned a bit and blew a fuse. So I took out the screwdriver, ice, and potatoes, and tried again. It groaned again; another fuse. I took out my watch and the artichoke heart and pushed the button. Another fuse. Then we just put in some water and it took right off, but the water loaded it down so much it started to smoke. We have heavy water in Washington, so I wasn't surprised.

We still have the blender somewhere. After spending that much money on it, no way was I going to get rid of it.

I remember when we purchased our first vacuum cleaner. I was reading *TV Guide* and noticed an ad that said, "New Vacuum Cleaner...Just $19.95." Since we were in the market for one, I answered the ad. The man who came to see us was from India and spoke with an accent, so I immediately began thinking about the starving millions in Calcutta, whom he apparently represented. He did nothing to make me think differently. Here was one of those millions — right in our living room.

The machine he brought in with him didn't exactly look like the one I saw in the ad, so I mentioned this to the salesman. The look on his face made me shudder, and I had a vague feeling he might get sick right there in our living room. He explained that the vacuum in the ad was one an older lady had brought back. And while it was a fine one, he really recommended that we buy the super model that he wanted to show us. Silly us.

We STILL wanted to see the $19.95 model, however, so he limped back to his truck and brought in an ugly, yellow, dirty machine that coughed when he plugged it in. It deposited new dirt instead of picking up the old. We, too, got sick looking at this machine, so I asked him to bring the other one back in.

He skipped back to the truck and brought in the beautiful, sleek canister-type we had first seen. This machine not only didn't leave any extra dirt, but it also sucked up steel balls, nails, and a hammer. It made bald spots in the rug, and I had to grab one of the kids before they got sucked up too. That was enough. We were sold — "How much is it?"

As I remember, it was $270 or so. We explained that we could never afford that much, thanked him for his demonstration, and said goodbye. But an amazing thing happened. He said he had forgotten about the February discount taking $100 right off the top.

One hundred seventy dollars was still more than we

could afford, and we told him so. But then he remembered we were entitled to a demonstration allowance which brought the price down another hundred.

So we bought it. And do you know, we are still using that machine over thirty years later, though by our calloused attitude we probably caused that poor guy to go back on the streets of Calcutta. It's hard to live with that on your conscience, but I guess I'll make it.

SOLUTION:

Don't read *TV Guide*.

PART II

THE
ROAD
I TRAVELED

SINGING
FOR SUPPER

BEFORE I TELL YOU MORE horror stories about trying to give up control of my life, let me give you some of my background.

I was born in Seattle, raised in Tacoma, and spent my childhood summers on a farm near Coulee City, Washington. I settled my family in Seattle, and will probably be here the rest of my life. How's that for a quick biography?

I have a wonderful dad. He's saved almost everything he's ever owned or found since he was four years old. He has a garage the Smithsonian wants when he's ready to give it up. I had the time of my life growing up among its treasures — such as a right rear fender for a Hupmobile (good to have in case Hupmobiles ever come back), the fan belt for a 1923 Model T, the left rear throwout bearing for a 1948 Jeep, one of every nut and bolt General Motors ever made, and a spare 1932 Model A motor which Dad kept under the workbench. You simply never know when someone is going to stop you and ask if you have handlebars for a

1937 Harley motorcycle, but Dad will be ready when it happens.

My mom was also just about perfect. One of her few failings was wanting Dad to clean out the garage, which Dad couldn't understand. Didn't she know that stuff was worth money? And anyway, what would he tell the Smithsonian? The proof of Dad's wisdom came once every three or four years when he would fix a faucet or a window latch or the furnace with something he had saved since high school. Mom would be so pleased to have it fixed, but I never really thought she had a true appreciation for what would have happened if Dad hadn't hung onto that particular bolt or screw.

And then there was the car. When Dad drove it, it ran perfectly (as he would point out in a firm voice). But Mom would often complain about the latest noise or leak. What did Dad do? He would fix it, of course; in just a few months he would get right to it. He was really busy at the shop and didn't have time to be coming home every ten seconds to fix Mom's car. Once Dad discovered, however, that the problem was the ringlenoffitt and not the grindandshafter, he would repair it rather quickly (luckily it was only the ringlenoffitt; otherwise it would have involved a major overhaul).

Dad used to take me to grade school in his Model A Ford. The school was about a mile from home. If I sat real still and didn't say anything, he would drive right past it and on toward work. Pretty soon he would wake up to the fact I was still in the car, and backtrack to the school and let me off. He always seemed amused by this — which I regard with wonder, since if my kids had done that to me I probably would have been bent out of shape with anger. I'm always in such a hurry.

My earliest memory of school was a snowy day in kindergarten at Franklin Grade School in Tacoma. I saw all the "big boys and girls" taking off their boots and hanging up their wet coats, and I remember wondering if I would ever be that big. They seemed so confident and important, those first-graders! The next thing I remember is graduating from kindergarten and going into first grade.

I cried a lot in the first grade, or at least was on the verge of tears much of the time. I've always had a sensitive spirit and even now things easily move me to tears. I never watch animal movies. I love horror stories, however, and can handle monsters eating people in the basements of dark castles. But when it comes to real-life situations I worry about people and animals being mistreated. I'm reading a book now about aliens zapping people with ray guys, but one of the main characters is a dog. I'm about to toss the book because I'm afraid the dog is going to get hurt in some way. Dumb? Probably, but that's just the way I am. Barb wants me to watch a Black Stallion movie on tape. No way! I'm sure a cruel owner or a tragedy in the horse's life will make me cry, and I feel weak when I cry.

It's funny the things you remember from school. One of my pals in fourth grade, Chuck Williams, stuck a pencil on the chair just as I sat down and the lead went into my flesh and broke off. The teacher had to take me into the hall closet and pick it out with a needle. How mortifying! I also remember the big boys talked and laughed about things in the bathroom that didn't make much sense, but I laughed too wanting to be a part of the "in" group.

I loved soccer. After a summer of baseball, one day we would put away our bats and out would come the soccer balls. No bells were rung. It was not on anyone's calendar, as far as I know. We just knew baseball was over and soccer was in. You would have been a nerd to continue playing baseball during soccer season, and nobody wanted to be a nerd!

Then there was the time I spilled hot chocolate in the lunchroom and Rosemary Bowe, one of the big sixth-graders, helped me clean it up. She was so nice and helpful, and didn't bawl me out. She later married Robert Stack, the movie star. I'm not sure how that applies to our conversation other than to let you know I have an "in" down in Hollywood if you ever need it.

Then came the big day when I went to junior high for the first time. What other heights could one possibly attain?

How big can you get? What else is there to learn? On the other hand, it was threatening too. My first shock came when I went into the lunchroom with my brown bag and saw teachers right in the same room with us, and they were eating! I couldn't believe it. They actually ate food! I assumed teachers were in the classroom all the time — days, nights, and holidays. They didn't have families or eat or drive cars or laugh at jokes. But here they were, having fun right in front of everyone. There were even rumors that the metal shop teacher smoked.

I also began to notice strange looking people who always knew the answer in class and could write it on the blackboard. They were called girls. They had long hair and wore dresses.

School was easy for me. I learned to give the teachers what they wanted, whether I understood it or not, and that seemed to satisfy the system. Most of my book reports were on chapter seven. "The part I liked best was in chapter seven, where Todd Forthright lost his way on the trail and the wolf..." I figured if the teacher thought I got all the way to chapter seven, he or she would assume I finished the book. I was too smart to give my report on the first or last chapter. Chapter seven seemed just about right, and was the only chapter I ever read. (The first book I remember finishing was one I read in the Army when there wasn't much to do.)

I can't remember anything negative from childhood about my home or the way my parents treated me. Some of my most delightful memories are of the times my mom and I played horseshoes, or when the family played indoor games in the evenings. I was, however, a little overprotected, as many firstborns are. I think that might have had something to do with the low self-confidence I had in my earlier years. I remember walking down the streets of my hometown, feeling sure others were looking and laughing at me. At school, if I saw a group of kids laughing in a corner, my first thought was that I was the target of their ridicule.

In hindsight I guess I wasn't being laughed at, because I was elected president of this and chairman of that, and became student body president and leader of the young people's group at church. It proves again, I suppose, that a person does not have to be unloved and misunderstood to lack self-confidence. Sometimes, as in my case, I think these uneasy feelings actually contribute to higher achievement.

My low self-confidence did keep me out of sports, however. One of my physical education instructors in high school put us through some running drills, and he said I had the makings of a terrific football player — loose hips, or something like that. On the day of the tryouts, as I was walking to the field, one of the older kids who was already on the squad said something like, "YOU are going out for football?" I mumbled something, and after he went on I headed home instead of to the field — an NFL superstar nipped in the bud.

In a talent show on my last day in high school I played my guitar and sang, and got a standing ovation. Kids came up to me afterward, amazed that I could do anything like that, and asked why I had waited so long to perform. I just said "Thanks," and thought about what might have been if I had only felt a little more sure of myself.

College was a little threatening because I didn't know anyone and really didn't know how to talk to strangers. I liked girls a lot better than boys, and had a lot of girl "friends," but none of the smoochy kind. I worshiped from afar, without the courage or knowledge to make any real advances. I had plenty of successes in my college years, but deep down the old nagging self-doubt kept rearing its ugly head.

I decided to seek a degree in veterinary medicine because I love animals. I'm forever escorting spiders outside who get trapped in the sink, or tipping beetles right side up, or fishing bumblebees out of the water. But one day I saw a note on a bulletin board in the dorm requesting a guitar player for a country music band. It was not my nature to push forward at all, but with the success of my last day in high school still ringing in my ears, I thought I would give it a shot. I auditioned and won a spot in the band.

Soon we were playing for Grange meetings and various groups on campus. Then we got our own radio show and even made some television appearances. It was so exciting I changed my major to communications, and eventually settled on a degree in radio and television. On what slender threads some of our major life decisions hang!

Sunday meals were not included in board bills at the dormitory, so that was the day I would often take the band to one of the sororities on campus. This gave us a free dinner with the girls, after which we would entertain them with our music.

On one of these sorority visits near the end of my junior year, I sat across the table from an attractive young lady named Barb. Just after dinner, however, a six-foot-ten, good-looking John Wayne-type football player came in and took that little doll out for the afternoon. (Barb told me later he was actually a five-foot-eight folksinger.) Giving up easily, as I usually did where girls were concerned, I made a mental note of Barb, but held little hope for any future contact. I figured she was taken, so I just put her on the shelf with all my other unfulfilled dreams. Barb told me later she went home that evening to telephone her mother and tell her she had just met the man she was going to marry — me, not the football player.

Two weeks later we both attended a Bible conference at a camp near Seattle. I was co-chairman of the conference, and could choose whatever discussion group I wanted to be a part of. I just "happened" to place myself in the group Barb was in.

Then tragedy struck. My only pair of shoes got wet, and I decided to make a quick trip home that night and get some dry ones. "Barb," I said, "would you like to ride to Tacoma with me so I can get some dry shoes?" I don't know where that kind of courage came from. Also I wasn't sure how Mom would react to my having a girl in the car after midnight, when the closest thing to dating I had experienced was taking some chocolate chips to a girl named Jean when we were in second grade, plus brief flirtations with a couple of hired girls on the farm.

But the trip was a success — Barb and I were engaged by the following Friday, and quickly began planning our wedding. Once I got the hang of it, I guess I could move fairly fast.

After the conference, Barb agreed to let me drive her to her home in Wenatchee. On the way we stopped to stay overnight at my folks' place in Tacoma. I still remember the next morning as I was sitting in the living room, and Barb appeared — in a dress! I had never seen her in a dress. I gazed in awe: Just think! I've brought home a real live girl to meet my folks, the kind I've read and dreamed about. Perfect! (I still get butterflies just looking at Barb — there have been lots of rough spots along the way in our marriage, but I know God gave me the perfect girl to be my wife.)

From there we had a great trip over the mountains to her home, driving a 1940 Studebaker that Dad helped me fix up. One of the few things Mom had succeeded in making Dad throw away was a door latch for a 1940 Studebaker glove compartment, and whenever Barb and I went over a bump, the door would fall down and bang her on the knee. Many times during the trip I would hear the click, and reach over and catch the door just before it hit.

As we drove up, I heard raucous laughter coming from Barb's house. I was sure they were laughing at me, but how could I disappear now without Barb noticing it? I worked up courage, got out of the car, and followed Barb inside, where 482 of her family members were jammed around the dinner table. The opening and closing of the glove compartment had made us late, so they were already eating. Barb's dad had been telling a joke (so they said). After they quit laughing at me, I sat down to dinner with them.

Barb's mother is really strange. She fixes the oddest things to eat, like cooked broccoli, pickled beets, salad with string beans in it, corn on the cob, tea, and other foreign dishes. Fortunately I discovered early in life that if I bit off six or seven rows from the corn cob, I could turn that side up and cover the rest with some lettuce from the salad, and it would appear I had enjoyed my meal (until they cleared the dishes, and by then it was too late). Also I found I could put fifteen teaspoons of sugar in the tea, and choke it down by holding my breath and taking small sips.

After dinner two of Barb's small nephews began bugging me to go out and play ball with them. This would mean leaving my precious Barb for a few minutes, but I knew my sacrifice would be good PR with her folks. It also would get me out of visiting with the rest of the family. So I got up and went outside.

Back in the kitchen, I later learned, Barb's brothers were giving her a bad time about bringing home her "cowboy." Betty, Barb's sister-in-law and always her protector, threatened to pour a pitcher of water over her husband's head if he didn't quit teasing Barb. Just as she started to pour, he raised his head and broke the pitcher. Outside I suddenly saw him dash from the house screaming, blood all over his face, and his wife chasing him with what appeared to be a broken pitcher. I wondered if I could possibly survive further contact with Barb's crazy family, but once again concluded there was no way to leave without her noticing.

Back at school that fall for my senior year, I was going in fifteen different directions at once, just as I have continued to do through the years. We even had a hard time finding an evening when we could officially announce our still-secret engagement (Barb hid her ring in her sorority mother's trunk).

Once the news was out, and knowing that people in the communications profession tend to lead hectic lives, one of my professors took Barb aside one day and asked, "Do you really know what you're getting into?"

"Of course," Barb replied. But she really didn't, and neither did I.

THE BEST
SPIT-BUCKET
EMPTIER

TWO DAYS AFTER WE WERE MARRIED, Barb and I were riding along in the car and I remarked to her, "I wonder what all this talk of adjustment is about anyway." We had heard that marriage would bring pressures requiring compromise and fine-tuning in our relationship. Since we had experienced no problems so far, I thought that type of thing must happen only in other marriages.

After graduating from college later that year I went into the Army, and became a second lieutenant serving in psychological warfare. We ended up at Fort Bragg, North Carolina, where, because they were short of officers, I filled a major's position as a battalion training officer.

One of my jobs was scheduling yucky things like the infiltration course, where vicious trainers parted your hair with tracer bullets as you crawled through the dirt. I also scheduled the gas chamber exercise where we learned who had the defective gas mask, and the field exercise where we were introduced to every local gnat and fly, and had to shave in cold water, using our steel helmets as a sink. A little confession is good for the soul, so I'll tell you that luckily I was trained in the Signal Corps, and knew where the electric plug-in was on the generator and could use my electric razor. The generator was so loud it covered up the razor's noise.

As training officer I also suggested to my colonel one summer that the above-mentioned exercises be delayed until October, when the weather in North Carolina is more pleasant. The colonel agreed. One slight coincidence is that I would be discharged in September. (Now that they know this, I hope they don't make me take Army over again.)

I really didn't understand the Army anyway. I was supposed to be training people in psychological warfare, but it seemed that someone was always wanting the men busy picking up pine cones or straightening the lines in the dirt under the barracks or policing (picking up) cigarette butts. I decided to find my fortune elsewhere.

We had two children by then, compliments of the Army. (Thank you, taxpayers! Tim cost us $7.50, and Bev cost us $25, which proves something you already knew: Girls are much more complicated than boys.) Returning to Seattle, we heard that a new television station was going on the air in a few months, so we decided to wait and see if that would provide me a job in my field. Meanwhile I worked in an apple warehouse and stewed.

One day Kit Spier from the top Seattle station, KING-TV, called me and offered me a try-out for a job as floor director. Another man would be competing with me for the job. I was put to work painting and arranging sets, cueing actors, and other interesting assignments. I worked hard at all of it. Thrilled and honored to be there, I even offered to do extra things, not just to make points but because I liked to keep busy.

We were doing a boxing show at the time called "King's Ring." The station's carpenter built a boxing ring right in the studio for the matches, and one of the floor manager's duties was to empty the boxers' "spit bucket." I took the task in stride with all the other duties, but I'm told my competitor didn't. When the try-out was over, I got the job — I guess they wanted the man who could empty the best spit bucket.

On my first full day on the job after the try-out, I remember standing beside a TV camera with one of my idols just a few feet away — Charles Herring. There I was, a farm boy from Tacoma and Coulee City, working with the most popular newscaster in the Northwest. I was in shock for days, because he treated me just like a person, winning me by his warmth and good humor. From Charles Herring I learned to be a professional.

Also at the station were Ted Bryant and Casey Gregerson, two people I had gone to college with. Now they had made it "big" on TV, but they still showed genuine concern for me and seemed to enjoy having me there.

After meeting many of these "important" people over the years I've learned that the really important people usually don't act like it. They are unassuming and ordinary. It's the folks who are still on the way up who seem to have the superiority complex.

One of my first jobs was to put the Alka-Seltzer in the glass at Mr. Herring's side while he gave the last news story before the commercial. He always led into the commercial by holding up the glass of fizzing Alka-Seltzer. It was my responsibility to make sure it was fizzy at the right time. The camera would change to a close-up of Mr. Herring while I crawled into the set on my hands and knees, dropped a tablet into the glass of water, then crawled back out.

One day the director got busy and forgot to cut to the close-up lens. I was new and didn't know a close-up lens from Mount Rainier, so I proceeded to do my usual thing — only this time the whole Northwest watched me crawl into the news set. I didn't get fired, since it wasn't my fault. But it did make another interesting memory for all of us — just like the live commercial we did for a linoleum company, where we put too much ink and grease on the surface and it just smeared when we tried to show how easily it would wipe clean, or the "breakless" china that broke, or the "easy starting" lawnmower that never would.

We also did shows from various local manufacturing plants. For one of these programs my job was to cue a man to pull a chain which would hoist a huge fish out of a tank. The man was Japanese. I carefully explained to him what he was to do, and he nodded and bowed. I assumed he understood me. Then we went live, and the time came to cue the fish person. I did, and nothing happened. He just nodded and bowed. I cued him once more, but again he nodded and bowed. As I found out later, he understood only Japanese — so we never did get the fish out of the tank.

Another one of my TV idols was Stan Boreson, a kids' show host. We hit it off right away. I began appearing on his show as a singing Victrola. We wrote our own songs and had a marvelous time. After I became a director I was assigned to his show. We would meet about 3:30 each weekday afternoon to prepare for a 5 P.M. show. Talking, laughing and planning, by 5 P.M. we had a show on the air that seemed to appeal to all ages. I took Stan's place on the air from time to time during his vacations, which was a terrific training experience for doing my own TV commercials and programs later. In fact, my whole experience at KING-TV was like going through school — I learned production, editing, and direction.

After a while I moved into middle management, overseeing all the station programming that wasn't live. I felt like I was shuffling a lot more paperwork than I really wanted, but I had a secure future with the company and enjoyed my associations.

On August 6, 1968, however, after almost eleven years at the station, with no other job in sight and with a wife and kids who still liked to eat regularly — I wrote out my resignation. Someone had something else for me to do.

4

STUNNED

WHILE I WAS GROWING UP, my parents always insisted I go to church. But I had little to do with God back then, and the Bible was a blank book to me.

Most of the pastors and teachers I knew didn't seem to be part of the real world. They gave me the impression they had perfect marriages, perfect children, and perfect thoughts, and spent two hours every day reading the Bible plus three hours in prayer. They would be shocked to think a "Christian" would ever have the kind of struggles I had, so when I had a problem the last person in the world I thought about going to for help was a pastor or Sunday school teacher. They just wouldn't be able to understand.

When I went away to college, I attended church occasionally out of guilt, and once in a while when I got into trouble I had a passing conversation with God, but nothing too meaningful.

After I was married and stationed at Fort Bragg, Barb and I began to attend church in nearby Fayetteville. A young pastor there gave me my first glimpse of the joy a Christian could have. Before that time I had the impression that the Christian life was only something to be endured.

At first, Barb and I were 11 A.M. Sunday Christians. Later we began attending a young couples' Sunday school class because of the overwhelming warmth the couples showed to us. Then we were asked to become leaders of a young people's group called Jet Cadets that met on Sunday evenings. *How much can the Lord expect me to do?* I thought. *Imagine! Going to church twice on Sunday!*

Then came my eleven years at KING-TV after our return to Seattle, and the August evening when I penned out my resignation. Although God didn't write anything to me on the walls or speak out of the clouds, I knew positively that He was impressing on my spirit the decision to resign — because *He* had something else for me to do.

It was a bit difficult explaining the decision to co-workers and friends. Few of them understood what I meant when I talked about "God's will." And I couldn't really explain. I just had to leave — that much I knew.

I had taken Advertising 101 in college, so I thought I might try that as my next career stop. I had never written a commercial, though I had directed the filming of many. And I had never shot a foot of film, other than for a church film I did with a rented camera. Yet suddenly I was thinking about entering a field where both these skills were mandatory for success.

At KING-TV I had directed commercials for a one-man ad agency whose accounts included a local grocery store. The man was a little threatened by the station's sales department, so when he had a film or slides he wanted to view, he would come in the back door of the station to my office and ask me to help him run the projector. I always did what I could to help him. After I left KING I had lunch with him and asked if he knew of any advertising agency that needed help. He said *he* could use some help. So I went to work for him as his production director.

He was a fine, moral, honest man, and, humanly speaking, I owe my entire career in advertising to him. I learned much at his feet, but was frustrated time and again at not being able to really please him with what I did. He would often tear apart the copy I wrote, which of course was his privilege as the boss. My goal was to please him, but I always seemed to fail.

Once I took some of *his* copy from the previous year out of the file, typed my name on it, and presented it to him. He tore that apart as well. I concluded he just had a hard time letting go of anything, and after learning that, I didn't take his criticism so personally.

Everyone else seemed pleased with my work, so I kept trying to do the best job I could for our clients and to grow in experience as well as in personal maturity, though I was miserable on occasion. Sometimes I would go home in tears and tell Barb I just had to get out of there — go back to KING, go out on my own, pump gas, dig ditches...anything to get out of what I was going through. That was when I learned we sometimes have to separate God's will from our emotions. I wanted to leave, but had no peace in my heart to go. It was almost as if God were saying, "Stick with it. I have some exciting plans for you later, when you complete this phase of your training."

Despite my frustration, the Lord continued to help me each day at the agency. I began taking on more and more responsibility and learning valuable lessons that I would apply later in my career.

One day the owner's wife stopped to talk with me as I was preparing to leave work. She said she and her husband were thinking about taking things a little easier, and wanted me to have the agency when he retired, since they had no family of their own.

Later one Sunday afternoon I received a phone call from the owner's wife, who in a strange tone of voice asked me to come to her house right away. Knowing something was wrong, I wasn't overly surprised to learn when I arrived that the owner had died.

The owner's widow, the secretary and I tried to carry on

as a partnership, but it just didn't work out. I offered to leave, but neither of the other two had the necessary background to carry on. So I bought the agency from the widow, and began to pick up the pieces and keep going as the owner had wanted me to, only now I was paying for the business rather than inheriting it.

A number of people asked me why I didn't just walk away, since the agency had no value apart from the people it employed and a few desks, typewriters and filing cabinets — there was no heavy equipment and no product inventory. In response, I told them I felt an obligation to help the owner's widow, who appeared to have nothing except the house she was living in. I think the Lord honored that decision. It was a good testimony to my Christian as well as my non-Christian friends.

At the time I thought little about future expansion and where I wanted the company to be in ten years. I was busy just trying to stay afloat. The company books indicated a bank balance of $3,000, but we discovered the account was actually empty. Nevertheless, it felt good to have our own business, and at least we weren't in debt to start.

My clients seemed to be happy as I wrote all their ad copy and bought commercial time for them, but I was sure there was more to the business than what my common sense was telling me. Less than a year after the agency's previous owner died, I attended a meeting of people from local radio stations and ad agencies at which the discussion topic was "What an Advertising Agency Does." One of the biggest agencies in town was putting it on. I was so excited — finally I would learn what I was supposed to be doing.

With pad and pencil in hand, I listened as the agency president got up after lunch and said something to the effect that "I'm just the president — I really don't know what we do, so I will now call on my vice president to tell you." The vice president got up and, though not in these words, indicated that "I just handle the finances. I don't know what we do either. I will now call on our creative director to tell you." The creative director got up and called on the media director.

All I saw were dollar signs. I thought, *You mean I have to pay all these people before I even sit down to the typewriter?* I decided right then to stay small and do much of the work myself, and not have a bunch of important folks running around wanting to be paid.

I also thought it was important to have a Christian testimony in my business, but Barb was always far ahead of me spiritually. She stayed at home while the kids were small, and found time each day to read the Bible. This helped her grow. Since the Bible was still a dull, dry book to me, I simply went through the motions of being interested in church to please her and, in a way, to keep from disappointing my parents. I served on church boards, taught Sunday school and junior church, and was blessed in a limited way. But spiritually, down deep, I was still a baby Christian.

You might argue that at this point I was not really a Christian. But I wouldn't agree. I had received Christ as my personal Savior, and believed that He was God, that He was born a man, that He died as the sacrifice for my sins and then rose alive from the grave, and that He was now preparing a place for me in heaven. There is no doubt in my mind that I was a born-again Christian. I was bound for heaven. I had lots of hope and security. But my focus was mostly tomorrow rather than today. I tried to love my neighbor who stared out the window at us, to relate to my boss, to communicate with Barb and my kids, and to deal with the people at church. But it was all on my own. I didn't have much of God's power at the time.

And I simply had never gotten into the Bible, which was the spiritual food I needed to grow. I had no one in my life with the time, inclination or knowledge to take me under their wing and help me grow. I didn't have a compelling desire to grow and to study on my own — or, if I did, I lacked the tools to do anything about it.

Barb continued to grow spiritually, and she always had the Bible and other Christian books lying around the house in plain sight. I tried to read a couple of her books, but I felt the authors had their heads in the sand and couldn't relate to

the world I lived in. They talked about *my* problems, all right
— but gave me the impression that they themselves had it
made, spiritually speaking, and why was it taking me so long
to get to where they were? I felt they were trying to put me
on a bunch of guilt trips.

So I didn't read Barb's books. Though they probably
would have been good for me, I wasn't comfortable with
things that were "good for me," like asparagus and the Bible.
I thought I was fine just the way I was.

One day a friend of mine, George Toles, gave me a book
to read. I could fake others out when it came to reading
Christian books, but I was afraid George would actually ask
me later how I had liked this one. I figured I would have to
read at least enough of it to give him the "part I like best"
answer that I had used in book reports in high school and
college.

I tried several times to get into the book, each time
putting it down again for a few more weeks, then trying it
once more.

One day I finally made it past the first chapter — and I
was stunned by what I read.

The book was Keith Miller's *The Taste of New Wine*. I was
sure Keith Miller must have been reading my mail, he knew
me so well. And he caused my whole spiritual world to open
up.

Here was an author who seemed honest about his feelings. He actually said he failed once in a while. Can you
imagine a Christian admitting that? When he mentioned his
problems they were not in the past tense. He was in the present-day process of working on them. I hadn't been able to
relate to Christian speakers I heard who said something like
"I *used* to get angry a lot, but now that I've been to seminary
it's in the past," or "I once had a problem with lust, but I
could read *Playboy* now and it wouldn't bother me at all," or
"We used to have conflicts in our marriage, but now it's been
years since we had a fight." Now I finally had found a Christian who had problems today just like me — and he indicated that God had answers.

I consumed that book and immediately read the three others Keith Miller had written at the time. He said astounding things like, "Sometimes I don't feel God is very close," or "Sometimes I don't feel like going to church," or "Sometimes I don't feel like praying," or "Sometimes I want God to leave me alone." Now I knew there were at least two of us on planet Earth who sometimes felt that way.

But Keith didn't leave me with his problems. He also told me how his life was being filled up with Christ, how the tears flowed so easily when he reflected on Christ's sacrifice for his sins, how Christ had given him a reason for living, the blue in his sky, the gold in the sunset, the hope, security and contentment he felt. He was God's own son too.

I longed for that same closeness to God that Keith Miller talked about. So I began my own search for the secret of his success that he had found through Jesus Christ.

5

A TASTE
OF ROAST BEEF

ONE DAY THE MAN who maintained our copy machine at the advertising agency stopped by to drop off some supplies. He told me about a speaker who was coming to town that summer to do a "Basic Youth Conflicts" seminar, whatever that was. I was not "into" seminars, especially a youth-type seminar. I politely told Harvey Edds I wasn't interested, just to get him off my back.

Harvey just kept smiling as I explained why I couldn't go to the Basic whatever-it-was. I was much too busy. Then he told me it would take every evening for a whole week! That settled it. I could never make time for that. My back ached twenty minutes into a sermon at church. How could I sit for a whole week? Finally I gave in and told Harvey to send me the materials, though I had no intention of going.

Harvey was wiser than I gave him credit for. He simply stooped to one of the lowest tricks known to mankind. He appealed to my ego. He casually mentioned that Bill Gothard, the man doing the seminar, was thinking about putting it on television and needed someone to give him some "expert" advice about it.

What Harvey said turned out to be true. Bill Gothard WAS thinking about putting the Basic Youth Conflicts seminar on videotape and needed some advice. I'm sure he could have found someone with more clout than a small-time operator in Seattle, but I was an expert of sorts and might be able to offer some of the needed help.

As I met with a few of the people involved and talked to Mr. Gothard on the phone, I decided the only way I could find out how to put the seminar on tape was to attend the dumb thing — every evening for a week! I made plans to attend, and Barb, of course, was happy to go along with the "TV expert."

Then I received a second shock. The seminar took up not only every weekday evening, but all day Friday and Saturday as well! I couldn't imagine spending that much time sitting, especially listening to a bunch of "sermons." How could I exist through that much preaching? I figured I could take some books to read, or wear earphones and listen to music, or maybe take up knitting.

When we went to the coliseum to register for the seminar, I was given a large red notebook with several blank pages for notes. Boy, was it red! You could see someone carrying it under his arm ten blocks away. Maybe if I put my coat over it, no one would know where I was going. And fat chance I would ever take any notes! What a waste of paper.

As we entered the auditorium for the seminar's first session, I was shocked to see more than five thousand people there, with just about every seat occupied, including those nearest the speaker. (*Imagine actually choosing to sit close to the front!* I thought. *That's a good way to get called on to pray, or to recite your latest memory verse.*) Fortunately, we were able to find seats up near the rafters where I was a little more comfortable.

Far below us on stage I saw this tiny person standing by an overhead projector. He spoke with a soft voice. "O Lord," I said, "this is going to be harder than I thought." But at least with that many other people around, I could hide.

I gave my attention that first night to finding suitable camera locations and wondering about audience reactions and how to anticipate them. People were actually laughing at some of the things Bill Gothard was saying!

By Tuesday I began listening to him myself — partly because I hadn't brought any books to read or music to listen to, and because I hadn't learned to knit yet. Soon I was listening intently. My focus was no longer on camera positions and audience reactions, but on Christ — the One for whom I had been searching so long, with no real hope of ever finding Him in a practical way.

I can't remember even a single twinge of back pain as I sat in the seminar for those thirty hours, soaking up this new and practical message. From a spiritual standpoint, it was the most important week of my life. By Saturday night my life was changed. It was as if I had found a secret exit from a dark forest, and the splendor of daylight unfolded as I stepped out.

This baby Christian who had lived on milk had finally tasted roast beef, and spiritual growth began in earnest.

PART III

LIGHTS COMING ON

6

A BETTER SPLIT

PERHAPS THE MOST IMPORTANT thing I learned from Bill Gothard's seminar was that God owned me 100 percent. Prior to that week, I had decided my relationship with the Lord would be an 89-11 split. I knew the Jewish people in the Old Testament were asked to give 10 percent of their resources to the Lord, and since I was no longer under law and had lots more advantages than they did, I thought I would be generous and give God another percentage point — a full 11 percent of my time and money. I expected God to be excited about my generosity, since I knew some people who gave Him only a dollar on Sunday.

But Bill Gothard's teaching made me realize God had paid a price for me (Jesus Christ on the cross) and owned not just 11 percent of me but all of me. That included not only my time and money but also my business, home, cars, family, and tennis ball machine.

Before I started reading the Bible, I always had the impression Christ had marched to the cross with banners flying, eager to pay the penalty for my sin. Now I learned that Jesus agonized in prayer on the night before His death, asking His Father if He could be spared from having to go through with it — yet He chose to do His Father's will. That made His sacrifice much more meaningful to me. In response to His unconditional gift, how could I do any less than make myself a "living sacrifice" as my "reasonable service" (as Romans 12 says)?

One thing that made me fear giving God control was that I thought He might lay some bad trip on me if He were running the ship. I felt I needed to keep a safe distance from Him — to sit in the back row, as it were — so He wouldn't get me into too many bad situations, such as going to a foreign country to be a missionary (I'm just an old farm boy — my preference is ham and eggs, not monkey tail soup or fried cobra fillets, with chopped turtle shell and ant eggs for dessert). Or I thought maybe God would have me play my guitar in the Salvation Army band, or make me wear thick glasses and pass out tracts on a downtown street, yelling at people about hell and the end of the world. Or, the worst possible thing of all, he might make me be a preacher. I'm sure you can understand why this made me so fearful.

But after I committed myself 100 percent to Christ on that Saturday night, I knew somehow that He would give me the grace to handle what He wanted me to do, and I told Him I would do His will whatever it might be — go to Africa, play in the band, or hand out tracts. There was only one exception: I would never teach or speak to groups — not in a million centuries! Since most of my teachers were people who seemed to "have it made spiritually" and didn't have problems, I knew I could never live up to that high calling. Besides I had a soft voice and got teary easily when I tried to communicate something very meaningful to me. I also hated preparing lesson plans.

I had a passion to know the Bible personally as something real and practical, but I didn't know anyone who knew how to make it come alive that way. In church I was taught such things as how the Jewish tabernacle was constructed, which direction the Hebrew tribes faced in the Book of Numbers, the meaning of the seventieth week in Daniel, and when the church started. I knew I was sanctified, glorified, justified, homogenized, pasteurized and sanitized — but no one had ever made the Bible practical to where I lived during the week.

When I gave the Lord the news that I would never teach, He got really excited. He was thankful I didn't plan to get in the way. He said He DID have some teaching and public speaking He wanted me to handle for Him, but since we both agreed I wasn't a teacher or speaker, then any success stories of people being changed through it would have nothing to do with me. It would have to be God doing it through me. All I had to do was keep my nose in the Book and show up. He would do the rest. So I began to build my message and teach, just as I said I would never do, and He has given me hundreds of opportunities to "practice."

However, here's just a bit of fatherly advice. It would be safer not to tell the Lord what you WON'T do. It didn't work for me.

Giving myself 100 percent to the Lord did not mean I had to sell everything and give the money away. What it meant was that I simply no longer had ownership of anything. I was a manager, not an owner. If God allowed our home to burn down, our car to be smashed, my wife to get cancer, or me to be crippled — or, on the other hand, if He let us have financial success, a good business, and good health — whatever He had in His plan for me, that's what I wanted to do or experience.

That didn't mean I just sat on my sofa and waited for God to do something. Even though God guides the Christian, He still wants us to try doors, fill out job applications, search the want ads for homes, send kids to college, put savings in a bank, buy insurance, and plan for retirement. We can't just sit around and assume God will take care of everything without any effort on our part just because we belong to Him. He likes action. It's much easier for God to change our direction if we are moving than it is to get us up off the couch.

One of the greatest tests of this is when we try to find a new job after being laid off. I counsel a lot of men who are going through this. As time drags on without results, their self-esteem and confidence get lower and lower, especially for those who are used to upper management positions. It's hard to fill out one more résumé or knock on one more door.

The first thing I check out is whether they are telling the Lord what they WON'T do. Most of the people in Seattle like it here. Those who are looking for a job find it natural to say "I'll take anything unless it involves moving away." But until they tell God, "I'm willing to go anywhere You want me to go...even Coulee City, or Kansas City, or Boston or Fargo," chances are He will shut all the doors in Seattle until they are able to make that commitment to Him.

He doesn't do this kind of thing to make us miserable. He just has a perfect plan for those who have made Him their focus in life. I would be stupid not to take help and advice from Someone who can see the future with twenty-twenty vision. When I trust His plan, I can go into that next job interview with my head held high, knowing the Lord has gone before me. He's checked out their books, checked out the people I would be working with, checked to see if my gifts match the job, and sat in the coffee shop and heard the gossip. If the interviewer says, "Sorry, we can't use you," I can leave that place singing praises to God. Why would I want to work somewhere He doesn't want me to be?

If you're facing a lot of closed doors, take inventory to make sure you're willing to go anywhere He wants you to go. You don't necessarily have to like the idea, but you have to be willing to learn to like it. That removes all the strings from God, and He gets excited working His plan for your life.

So often it's a step-by-step process to follow God's direction. The future might be a little dark, but He gives light for the next step. In the wilderness where the Jewish people wandered for forty years, archaeologists have found candle holders designed to be strapped around the ankle. A person wearing them at night would always have light for the next step so he could watch for rocks and holes and scorpions. With each step, he had light for the next one. I believe that's the way God leads us — at least that's been my experience. We look up and the future is dark. We look to His light (the Bible) and we clearly see the next step we should take.

At times the next step might mean doing NOTHING. Somehow we seem to feel we should always be moving in one direction or another. It's so hard just to wait and be quiet and still when nothing much is happening. My inclination at that point is to take the reins in my own hands and do things on my own. God lets me, too. He doesn't put a big roadblock in my way. He just says, "If you get in trouble, let Me know." And of course I do get in trouble, and at some point have to get back on His team.

When our kids were little, I can remember testing their understanding of traffic signals: "What does the red light mean?" (*"Stop."*) "What does the green light mean?" (*"Go."*) "What does the yellow light mean?" (*"GO FAST!"*) Oops — I guess I modeled the wrong thing. Yellow means go slow, and sometimes that's what we need to do in our decision-making.

I believe in burglar alarms and fire insurance. I don't build fires in the middle of the living room rug, or lie down in the path of a speeding train. God gave us common sense. But God's ownership of me means that after I have done everything in my power to do what God wants me to do or to protect His property, and still my plans don't go quite the way I want, I accept the circumstances as coming from God to teach me patience, to mature my character, or to give me the ability to love and help people as they go through similar struggles.

In effect, God filters everything that comes into our life through His hands of love. He knows what will happen to us. He sometimes even DESIGNS struggles to help mold us into the people He wants us to be. Then He gives us the tools to get through the problem, and thereby become valuable to someone else going through the same thing.

7

MY SERVE

THE SECOND MOST IMPORTANT CONCEPT Bill Gothard taught me (God's 100-percent ownership was the first) was that a Christian's highest calling is to be a servant. The highest calling!

My natural self doesn't want to serve. I want to BE served. I want to be noticed, to be important, to have my name mentioned, to be honored, to be first in line, to be president. A servant is not usually noticed or important or honored or first or president. A good servant is able to allow credit and honor to go to others, even for things the servant thinks up on his own.

Becoming a servant was not what I'd had in mind for my life. I like to have things done my way on my schedule, and I don't appreciate a bunch of people running around with opinions different from mine. In fact I wouldn't have any conflicts or problems if people would only keep their opinions to themselves and let me do it my way. When I wanted to shut others out, what a shock it was to discover God wanted me to do just the opposite — to serve them!

Before I attended the Basic Youth Conflicts seminar, I considered people to be a pain — at least some of them. I often told Barb the world would be a wonderful place if it didn't have any people in it. For me, the old saying was true: "If you want something done right, do it yourself." I thought I just didn't need anyone.

I also had schedules for everything. I knew what I was going to do this afternoon, tomorrow morning, and next year, and I knew pretty much what I wanted to accomplish in the next ten years or so. But as God began giving me teaching opportunities, He started bringing people into my life who messed up my schedule. I would be working on a very important project when someone would drop by with a simple case of divorce, cancer, death, or suicide, and expect me to stop everything I was doing and relate to his or her problem.

Then God began to soften me in this area of my life. The phrase "Circumstances are temporary; people are eternal" became my motto. I began to realize that the only riches we will transfer when the Lord comes or we die are the people we influence for Jesus Christ. Everything else in time will be dust — our schedules, goals, systems, commercials, homes, cars, money — just dust. Then an amazing thing happened. Little by little God began to help me love people, though actually HE was doing the loving through me, just as He promised.

The attitude of servanthood became my business philosophy. I try to serve my clients in ways they don't expect or request. Not just "service," but "serving." We can give service expecting something in return, focusing on what WE get out of the situation. On the other hand, when we are truly "serving" we focus on the OTHER person's needs and don't need to get anything back in return. I want to serve my clients just as Christ would if He were here in my place. I have learned over and over what a privilege it is to really serve.

My good friend Gary Smalley taught me a valuable lesson that has been reinforced to me from Scripture: *Love is an action, not a feeling*. Sometimes I do not feel like doing the right thing for Barb, my neighbor, my boss, or my kids. But because I know God would have me do a certain thing, I do it as an act of my WILL, not my feelings. My feelings can be exactly the opposite from what I KNOW God wants me to do. However, an interesting thing often happens; the right feelings come AFTER I have done what I know God wants me to.

At times I've worked for clients who could be unfair, demanding, and unappreciative, and who gave me the impression I would be tolerated only until they found a better replacement. One day, one such man I was working for made another in a long series of threats. I went home to Barb and we went for a walk in the cemetery. I don't know why the cemetery, unless I thought I could hear God better since it's especially quiet there. We sat on some rocks, and talked over some things I already knew, but Barb reminded me that God's plan could not be messed up by anyone. If I lost the client, God knew all about it and had something better in mind. It was the first time I had ever hyperventilated — for no other reason than the stress of the moment, my breath came in big heaves and my heart pounded. I knew God had a plan and was in control, yet my mind rebelled at the thought of losing something for which I had worked so hard with so little reward.

In that cemetery, with Barb's help, I rededicated to the Lord my life, my career, my family, my material goods, my time, and my future, knowing His plan would be the best for me. I also knew God wanted me to honor and serve the client with all the strength I could muster. I began doing that by an act of my will, no longer fearful of what he could do to me. He couldn't do anything God did not allow. With this reminder, I began to respect, serve, and honor that guy — and when I did, God gave me the feelings of love I didn't have going into the situation. In time the man softened and began to honor me, and we became good friends. All I did was obey. God did the rest.

This was an amazing lesson that has helped me face similar situations since then. It was just one more confirmation that the Bible does have practical insights on handling our day-to-day relationships.

As I look back on those hard times, I'm sure I was communicating a resistant spirit to my friend at first, and it was resistance I got back — a reflection of myself. There will always be that type of person around, so the sooner we learn to focus on our own attitudes rather than on the other person's shortcomings, the better servants we are going to be. Only God can change another person's heart, and whether He ever does is His business, not ours.

8

THAT BORING BOOK

FOR SO MANY MANY YEARS I thought the Bible was dry as dust. The reason? I had never really read it.

Can you believe I rejected something I hadn't even read? That's downright intellectual dishonesty — like not believing in atoms because I've never seen any, or not believing there's a Peoria, Illinois because I've never been there.

The Bible really is an exciting book, but the Bible being presented in my church seemed pretty boring. So during the sermons I dreamed a lot: I took trips, and built furniture in my shop, and worked on business matters. Every now and then guilt pangs would force me to take the Bible down from the shelf when I got home, blow off the dust, and try once again to make it meaningful to my life.

The logical place to begin reading a book is at the beginning, so I would start in Genesis — and boggeth down somewhere around Noah. It simply didn't relate to where I lived, so I would put it back on the shelf. The next time the guilt pangs hit, I would turn to the New Testament. Right away I was in trouble because Matthew started his book with a bunch of "begats." Again it had no meaning, so back on the shelf it went.

At the Basic Youth Conflicts seminar, however, Bill Gothard said God could reveal everyday practical things through the Bible He had written. I knew it was up to me to test it out. So I began reading it. As I did, spiritual riches began cascading down on me at a dizzying pace. I was thrilled. Now even the Bible began to make sense!

Bill Gothard also introduced to me the principle of memorizing whole chapters of the Bible instead of just isolated verses where the context is not always clear. I also learned what it meant to meditate on God's Word. Meditation had always been a strange word for me. I could visualize a bunch of monks in a monastery somewhere chanting, "Ooo-ug-em-wowee-yum-look-um-phooey-to-youee." I'm not into chanting, so I didn't think I would be very good at meditation.

I learned, however, that meditation was simply repeating back to God His own words from the Bible. As we memorize Scripture we just repeat the message back to Him, and as we do, His principles become a very real part of our lives. They help us pre-program our minds to handle better our anger, negative thinking, financial difficulties, family problems, and other trials as they come up in our life.

The more we saturate our minds with biblical principles, the more we will react as Christ would when we encounter bad situations. Our ways are not God's ways. When someone curses us, we want to curse back at him; but God's Word says, "Bless him." We want to honor ourselves; God says, "Be a servant." We want to keep our money and spend it on ourselves; God says, "Give it away and I'll give you lots to give away."

Part of my problem in not understanding the Bible was that I had been trying to fathom the King James Version. It was the only translation I had way back in the olden days. Now please don't get me wrong. The King James is a wonderful version, and God has changed countless lives through its pages. Some people will not use any other translation, and that's okay; but I need things simple, and in my own language. The King James could be called "Good News for Seventeenth-Century Man." There is nothing sacred about the words "thee," "thou," and "verily." That's just how folks talked in the days when King James lived. It fact that's the way Shakespeare talked, and I can't recall anything too spiritual about his writings.

Barb had been reading something called *Living Letters*, a paraphrase by Ken Taylor of the New Testament epistles. Ken Taylor evidently had the same feelings I did, only he did something about it. He produced a Bible for his kids, and in the process changed my life. The *Living Letters* book didn't sound spiritual enough to really be a Bible, so I didn't pay much attention at the time. Then in 1971 *The Living Bible* was published for the first time as a complete work, and what an exciting day it was when I "discovered" it! Its simple, down-to-earth language was easy to understand.

Rather than starting in Genesis or Matthew, however, I decided to start in Romans (since it was the first book in the Bible by Paul, the missionary to the Gentiles — and, as far as I could figure out, I was a Gentile) and pick out just those

---

BRAND NEW MARRIAGE—One of the biggest things I learned by studying the Bible was how to be a husband to Barb. I thought I was doing great until I began to realize the awesome responsibility I have before God to be Christ to Barb. That means having His characteristics of gentleness, kindness, tenderness and unconditional love. I need to be a good listener, put Barb's needs first, make her my hightest priority. (Someone has said "marriage is not finding the right mate, but becoming the right mate." I think that says it all.)

These were all brand new thoughts to me. No one had ever told me much about these things, though I'd been going to church all my life. The complete story of my failures in marriage—and how we learned to be a true team—can be found in our book INCOMPATIBILITY: Grounds for a Great Marriage!

principles I could apply to my Monday-through-Saturday life
(I was pretty good on Sunday). I planned to put the few limited principles (maybe one or two per chapter) in a notebook
to copy and give to my friends who were having the same
struggles I had getting into the Bible. I also planned to type
out those few isolated principles and pin them on my bulletin board at the office so I could refer to them from time to
time.

To sort out those few items I would include in my personal version, I began underlining with a red pen just those
principles I could apply to my everyday life. I was amazed!
The pages began to drip red ink. In some cases, I was underlining almost every sentence in the chapter. And when I hit
Romans 12, I discovered an overflowing treasure of practical
guidelines:

> I need to give myself to God as a living sacrifice.
> Don't be caught up in the things of this world.
> Be a new and different person.
> God's ways really do satisfy.
> I need to be honest as I estimate my abilities.
> I have a special part to play in the Body of Christ.
> God has given me unique gifts to use in His service.
> I shouldn't just pretend to love people.
> I should hate what is wrong in God's sight.
> I need to delight in honoring other people.
> I shouldn't be lazy in my work.
> I should be patient in trouble.
> I need to help God's people when they are in trouble.
> I need to invite guests home to dinner in God's name.
> I need to share someone else's sorrows.
> I should not act big and important.
> I shouldn't think I know it all.
> I should not pay back evil for evil.
> I shouldn't quarrel with other people.
> I should not avenge myself.
> I should feed my enemies.
> I should conquer evil by doing good.

Fantastic! These principles hit me right where I lived!

I also learned from Bill Gothard that the depth of my message (getting into the Word of God) was my responsibility, while the width of my ministry (the number of people influenced by my life) was God's responsibility. As I started fulfilling my responsibility by putting my nose into the Bible, I would look up and see someone who needed exactly what I had been learning — the same principle that was impacting my life at that very moment. So I would share the principle, go back to the Book, and look up later to see ten people there, then eighty, then hundreds needing the very same principles I was learning, principles that made sense and could be applied to our everyday lives.

After I completed underlining a *Living Bible*, I would buy another one and start over. Each time I went through it I underlined passages I had skipped the previous time. I bought copies to put in my briefcase, in my car, in every bathroom at home — wherever I could get to them when I had a few minutes to spare. I had a copy of it at the office — in fact, a stack of them so I could give them away. I bought *The Living Bible* on cassette tape so I could listen to it while driving.

I fully realize *The Living Bible* is what's called a "paraphrase." This means it is a thought-for-thought rather than a word-for-word translation. For some people that's a problem and they should use some other translation. For me, however, that's an advantage. I want to find out what the Bible is saying — the thought behind the words — and then go out and see if it works. The basic thought behind each biblical concept is identical even though it might be expressed a little differently in various translations.

A former Seattle Seahawk football player came to know Christ personally at one of the pro athlete conferences we help with. He liked drugs and alcohol and assumed the thing to do after a game was go to the bar and get drunk. The next day he would observe some of the Christian players with bright eyes and smiles, and through his hangover he wondered if they ever had any fun. Now that he knows Christ personally, he is a supernaturally changed man, and is counseling others with problems in drug and alcohol abuse. He has different priorities and thoughts and morals, and does strange things like read the Bible and grow from it. If there were no other proof of God's existence, I would have to point to this man and hundreds of others I know just like him who have had an encounter with Jesus Christ and have been given new lives.

Christians aren't the only ones with faith. Everyone exercises faith at one time or another. When was the last time you saw the pilot on your flight to Denver or New York? We assume there is a pilot aboard, but we rarely see him. We hear his voice once in a while waking us up to mention the weather in Butte, but that could be a recording. We have faith he is not stoned out of his mind, that he has been to flight school and got passing grades, and that he knows what all those little switches in the cockpit are for. I would say it takes a ton of faith to put my life in the hands of someone I have never seen and will probably never meet face to face. I've never seen the wind either, but I have seen its effects. I have never seen Jesus Christ face to face, but I have faith that He exists because I have seen the difference He makes in my life and in the lives of others.

BIBLE
ON THE RUN

LOOKING BACK, I guess one of the things that kept me out of the Bible was the judgmental attitude of some Christians who made me feel I had to spend an hour each morning reading the Bible or I wasn't spiritual. For my lifestyle, I found that I had to do my Bible study in bits and pieces during my busy day. I would read the Bible when I found myself early for a meeting, or delayed in traffic, or waiting for someone at a restaurant. It became the focus for my spare minutes.

Every time I make a lunch date or schedule a breakfast, as I seem to do four or five times a week, I take along the Bible or some other Christian book I am reading. When people forget their appointments or get caught in traffic, I have a terrific time reading and learning.

Last year I made a breakfast date with a guy who wanted some counsel. I agreed to meet him at a restaurant located about midway between Seattle and Tacoma. I got up early that morning to make the trip, and it had snowed. I hate snow! It disrupts my schedule, makes me put on funny tires with nails in them, and prevents me from getting out of my driveway. So that morning I see I'm in trouble, but knowing I have to meet this guy, I go out in that miserable stuff and put on those dumb tires, and bang my frozen knuckles on the bumper jack that is always welded down underneath the spare tire, which is always covered with all the vital stuff I keep in the trunk.

I finally get those stupid tires on so I can get out of the driveway and begin the tortuous drive, sharing the freeway with all the jerks who haven't driven on snow since the winter of '23. They spin their tires and do sideway flips at sixty miles an hour. I enter this madness to meet this guy who made me drive one hundred miles out of my way to have a stupid breakfast where he probably won't take my counsel anyway! I have a telephone in my car, which is about the only thing that made sense that morning, and after I had almost completed the five-hundred-mile trip to the restaurant, it rang. I was informed my breakfast partner had called and cancelled the breakfast because he didn't want to go out in the snow! *Lord*, I prayed, *how much suffering can you expect one person to take?*

Well, I looked for the next exit, slid into a restaurant parking lot, slushed my way to the door, flopped down in a cozy booth, had a refreshing cup of coffee, put on my glasses, and began to read one of the books I kept in the car while I ate a nice warm meal, all by myself. And I learned a principle through my reading that I told about the following Sunday in the class Barb and I taught. Three or four people came up to me afterward to say the ideas I had shared were exactly what they needed to get them through the next week.

Circumstances? Chance? Coincidence? Not on your life! That episode was God-designed to test my patience, help mold my character, and force me to stop for a few minutes to learn a principle He wanted me to teach others.

It may be that trying to pick up scriptural principles in bits and pieces in restaurants, bathrooms, and briefcases won't work for you. Maybe you need to get into the habit of spending a certain amount of time reading each morning or evening. I don't think it really matters to God. I feel He will bless our efforts no matter what method we use to begin studying and applying His Word. It's our heart attitude that counts.

We need to remember to approach the Bible in a balanced manner. For instance, I have talked with people who try to appropriate every Old Testament promise into today's living. I also know people who almost throw out the Old Testament and spend all of their time in the New Testament. Some people study only the letters of the Apostle Paul, some only Paul's prison epistles. I think the answer to all this is given in what Paul wrote to Timothy:

> The whole Bible was given to us by inspiration from God and is useful to teach us what is true and to make us realize what is wrong in our lives; it straightens us out and helps us do what is right. It is God's way of making us well prepared at every point, fully equipped to do good to everyone. (2 Timothy 3:16-17)

Violating this principle is one of the reasons I feel some of the TV preachers have fallen in recent years. Their message centered mostly on evangelism and spiritual gifts. There was very little practical living in their message; no steak, just milk. The Bible says the church is not designed for evangelism. The church is to feed the "sheep" (you and me), and the sheep go out to the advertising agencies, plumbing shops, athletic teams, and board rooms to win people to Christ. We are just talking to ourselves if we major on salvation messages and gifts in church, never getting into the "meat" of the Word. The book of Hebrews points out:

> You have been Christians a long time now, and you ought to be teaching others, but instead you have dropped back to the place where you need someone to teach you all over again the very first principles in God's Word. You are like babies who can drink only milk, not old enough for solid food. You will never be able to eat

solid spiritual food and understand the deeper things of God's Word until you become better Christians and learn right from wrong by practicing doing right. Let us stop going over the same old ground again and again, always teaching those first lessons about Christ. Let us go on instead to other things and become mature in our understanding, as strong Christians ought to be. Surely we don't need to speak further about the foolishness of trying to be saved by being good, or about the necessity of faith in God; you don't need further instruction about baptism and spiritual gifts and the resurrection of the dead and eternal judgment. The Lord willing, we will go on now to other things. (Hebrews 5:12,14; 6:1-3).

The "meat" of the Word is practicing being a Christian. That means learning to handle anger, to love our wives unconditionally, to be patient with our children, to control our thought lives when we're on the beach, to be a good neighbor, to be a good servant, and to be a good steward with our finances. That's the meat. It's easy to major in the minors like church history and spiritual gifts. Those things don't threaten anyone or change lives. It's easy to trade cute Christian sayings like "love your enemy" — until you have an enemy staring you in the face. Do God's principles really work when we're under that sort of stress?

WHERE'S LIFE?—A friend of mine died quite young, and the funeral was held in a mainline denominational church. The religious leaders came in with their pomp and robes and pious faces and went through their ritual. Scores of my non-Christian friends from the media were there. I wanted to get up and scram, "THIS IS NOT WHERE IT IS FOLKS. THIS IS RELIGION. IT BORES PEOPLE. CHRIST IS REAL. RELIGION IS DEAD!" Of course I didn't, but I surely didn't want my friends to think what they saw there was what had changed my life. Far from it.

To be honest, I'm bored with heavy doctrine, church history and religion, but I couldn't be more excited about a relationship with Jesus Christ. There's a world of difference.

I never thought the Bible would be anything but a dull, dry book. I'm amazed at God's gift of helping me understand it. And then all I have to do is be obedient to the things I read on those pages.

It's not always convenient to study the Scriptures, with all the stresses and pressure of everyday life. I'm also sure Satan isn't all that anxious for us to read the Bible. He comes up with all sorts of distractions, but we have to keep at it, and make time for it, even if we think we don't have time.

What we do or don't do involves our priorities. We get the things done that are important to us. We may forget the dentist appointment, but hardly ever forget the tennis date. We might forget the committee meeting at church, but would never forget the aerobics class. Our priorities indicate our values. Other people can tell what is important to us by observing what we do.

But priorities change. It takes constant readjustment and fine-tuning. Right after I left KING-TV and began working in the small advertising agency, I started to produce films and slide presentations for various Christian organizations. I worked long hours on these and other projects, and I think they accomplished some good things for the Lord. But as I began getting into the Bible on a regular basis, my message began to deepen, and God started to bring all sorts of hurting people into my life and began phasing out my film ministry. Because I was into His Word, I sensed this adjustment in my priorities. I could have continued to do films — there is still a need for this type of service — but God had something better for me to do.

We phased out of teaching an adult Sunday School class recently because it became clear God wanted us to speak to different groups about the same subject (relationships) rather than speaking to the same group about different subjects. The class was a wonderful opportunity to help people, but our marriage seminars and writing became a higher priority, and we couldn't do both.

Our priorities speak so loudly they drown out our words,

and one of the priorities that will have a maximum impact on our lives is Bible study. You begin studying the Scriptures through an act of your will. Then God begins to shine a searchlight on the passage you are reading, and maybe for the first time in your life you too will become excited and blessed as God's Word comes alive before your very eyes.

10

'WHEEL-SPINNERS' AND 'YES, BUTTERS'

SOMEONE ONCE ASKED ME how I would go about trying to reach a person who didn't believe the Bible is true. I don't think it can be done, humanly speaking. All we can do is tell how the Bible has changed our lives. Until we have common ground, using the Bible as the final authority, it is almost impossible to have a meaningful discussion. Unless the Holy Spirit is at work in the person's heart, nothing will happen anyway.

I've learned it doesn't help to get into long, drawn-out discussions with people who don't want to grow. Christ even suggested that His disciples should "shake the dust off their sandals" when they found a city that was not open to their message. I run into people I call "Wheel Spinners" or "Yes, Butters" — "Yes, but I don't have time to get into the Bible." "Yes, but I don't feel like it." "Yes, but she did it first." "Yes, but you should see the way my boss treats me."

I've told a few people I could no longer help them because of their unteachable spirits. Why bang your head against a closed door when a hundred doors are wide open — people who are anxious, hungry, willing to learn and grow? We can waste a lot of time spinning wheels when we should just turn to the doors that are open. It's essential, however, that we be into the Bible on a regular basis.

After they've been exposed to all the denominations, cults, splinter groups and sects, non-Christians ask me, "How can I know which one is right?" Fortunately God has sent His Holy Spirit to minister to us as we read the Bible, and He will help us come up with the correct interpretation as we use good Bible study tools such as commentaries, various translations, dictionaries, and word study books. I suspect people who draw the wrong conclusions about Scripture passages have simply not gone far enough in their investigation. Most of the time they take only a cursory, shallow look at the meaning of a particular verse and jump to the wrong conclusions by not comparing Scripture with Scripture or taking into consideration the cultural aspects of that particular passage and its context.

It amazes me to hear people say, "I don't believe the Bible," or "It's full of myths," or "It isn't practical to my life," or "I can't understand it." Most of the people who say things like this have never read the Bible or made an honest attempt to see if the things in it are true.

I took astronomy in college. When I read about Saturn's rings, it would have been stupid of me to say to the teacher, "I don't believe it. That's just a fairy tale, there are no rings around Saturn," and then quit the class without looking any further. It's like saying, "I've never seen the rings, so they don't exist." That would be intellectual dishonesty.

I read the account of a college student who said to his professor, "I could never go along with Christianity because of the lack of credible evidence and the myths on which it was founded." The wise teacher didn't put the student down or get angry. She just told him she would be excited to review the details of his research, because he obviously must have examined the basic documents concerning Christ. "You mean the Bible?" asked the student. "Yes," replied the teacher. "It goes without saying we have to carefully investigate things like this before concluding they are false." At that point the student had to admit he had never read the Bible. He had just joined a crowd of people who were critical of the Bible but had never read it. They talked about the myths of the Bible, yet had never taken the time to see if the principles were right or wrong.

After thousands of years of challenge, the Bible has proved to be true and accurate in everything it has claimed. Such a record is a good indication to me that God was the author, not man. And as I've mentioned, even if I didn't have all the tangible evidence about the accuracy of the Bible, I would have to consider it a supernatural book because of the changes in lives I have seen it make. No one can argue with the difference in my own life — and in the lives of men and women all around me who have changed almost overnight after an encounter with Jesus Christ.

Occasionally I talk with a non-Christian who can't figure out why God had to become a man to save us. It reminds me of something I observed during the summers I worked on my Grandfather's farm. I used to go hiking in the sagebrush, looking for petrified wood. Occasionally I ran across a giant red ant hill. I'd always have some crackers and bread along to feed the birds, so I would stop and crumble some of the crackers or bread around the ant hill. Those ants would go out of their minds with this "manna" from heaven.

As I observed the ants, however, I saw they were not very smart. Two ants would argue over the same crumb of bread. Others would go way out of their way to get back to the nest. I would see ants struggling to climb rocks with bits of bread when they could have gone around the rocks much easier. I could have shouted, blown horns and sirens, stomped my feet, threatened them, rung bells, but there was no way they would even know I existed. Even if I stepped on a few of them, there would be no understanding of what had happened.

The only way I could take a message to those ants would be to become an ant. "Henry, you take that piece and let

Charlie take the other. Sally, don't go over that big hill; go around it. It's much easier. Joe, go straight to the nest, don't take so many curves." If my message made sense, they could relate to me as an ant and take my advice to make their lives better.

The only way God was able to bring a message to us was to become a man. The Bible is the story of that encounter of Christ with humanity, so it is essential that we read it to find out how this encounter can affect our lives — today and for eternity.

PART IV

ZOOMING IN

11

PORTRAITS OF PATIENCE

LET'S TALK A LITTLE MORE about the battle we controllers have with patience, which seems to be the hallmark of our struggles with life. Everyone and everything is out to irritate us by blocking our goals and doing things "wrong." Some guy up ahead wants to turn left, and there are 405 cars and trucks waiting behind him, including me. So what if that's his driveway? The least he could do is come home at a decent hour, or make a U-turn and come back on the other side of the street and turn right, instead of making people angry.

There's a red light on a street by our home that I've asked the city to remove. It's in a lonely part of the neighborhood, protecting a seldom-used street. In fact, only twice in recorded history has anyone come from the other direction. On May 14, 1933, Mazie Rathknocker lost her way up there before turning around and coming back out at the light. The other time was August 23, 1962, when Henry Radburner took the wrong turn, and had to come out. Other than those two

occasions, no one has ever used that street or needed the
light. So it irritates me to have to keep stopping there.

I go into the bank and see four lines, three of which have
58 people in them. The other line has only two people — an
innocent looking old lady, and a young boy. I opt for that
line. As it turns out, the lady is trying to cash a fifty-year-old
Social Security check she found in a drawer, and it takes a
series of calls to the bank headquarters in Oakland to get the
matter straightened out. Then the young boy presents his
penny collection, which will require five hours to count. By
now I realize why the 174 other people chose the other three
lines, though by this time they have all gone through, and
there are 174 new people in each line, one of which I join.

Even Barb tries my patience at times. I make instant decisions, but it takes her a while to make up her mind. For instance, Barb has a major decision pending which she should
have made before she was out of sixth grade, but keeps
putting off. It's the decision about whether she would rather
freeze to death or burn to death. She keeps wavering back
and forth, depending on whether it is winter or summer.

She's wavering on some other important issues too, and
until she makes these crucial decisions we are stuck at dead
center and can't proceed. We can't take our fifty-mile survival
hike until she selects the color backpack she wants. We can't
take the 10,000-mile RV trip until she decides what kind of
motorhome to buy, and whether she wants to cook three
meals a day or just two. We can't take the July motorcycle
ride through Death Valley until she decides between a Honda
or a Yamaha.

One of my dreams has been to build a "Chuckland"
amusement park here in the Northwest (we don't have any
Disney-type attractions here to speak of), and I have great
ideas for it. Big problem: Barb hasn't decided whether she
wants to take tickets in the morning and cook jam (like Mrs.
Knott at the berry farm) in the afternoon, or cook jam in the
mornings and take tickets in the afternoon.

You can name just about any area of my checkered life,
and I could say I have had (and still have) problems demon-

strating patience — with Barb, with bank lines, with red lights, with too many people driving on MY freeways, with too many people crowding MY restaurants, with road construction, with maps and instructions, and even with God sometimes, when He doesn't do things on my schedule.

The subject of patience reminds me of the young seminary student who went in to see his teacher and asked, "Professor, I'm having a terrible time with my patience. Would you pray that God would give me patience?"

"Of course," the professor replied, and he began to pray, "O Lord, please bring difficulty and tragedy and problems and trials and suffering into this young man's life. And may he face struggles with — "

"HOLD IT!" the young man cried. "I wanted you to pray for patience, not suffering!"

But of course, the old professor was right, because the only way we can learn to have patience is to go through trials that test our patience.

The first problem is that patience is a "fruit of the Spirit," so I need to spend some time in the Bible checking to see what God's attitude is about this struggle with patience that repeatedly plagues me.

So I've done that, and here are some of the Scripture passages He has shown me (in each passage, the italics are mine).

• • •

Rest in the Lord; *wait patiently* for him to act. (Psalm 37:7)

This is one of the hardest Scriptures for me to put into practice. We know God has a perfect plan for our life. We know His ways are not our ways. We know He sees the future with twenty-twenty vision. We know He wants the best for us. We know He goes ahead of us protecting and guiding us. But when the money doesn't come in on time, the cancer doesn't get cured on time, the house doesn't get sold on time, the job doesn't open up on time, the letter doesn't get here on time, the repairman doesn't arrive when he should, we get all upset and worry and fret and stew and wonder if God is really paying attention to our problem.

Notice that the first word in this verse is *Rest*. That's a toughie for me. I want to go out and take life by the throat and MAKE THINGS HAPPEN. *Rest* is a foreign word for me, even on vacations.

Because of our small business, we don't have a chance to get away much; but when we do, Barb likes to go somewhere and sit for a week. Since I know she needs this, I go along with a happy face and try to make the best of it. I'll take my computer and the latest book I'm writing just to make sure I have something to do. After I get to where we are going, work is not all that appealing, so I will read. I read sitting up, then read laying down, then read standing up, then read on the bed, then read on the couch, then read at the table, then sleep a bit, then read some more. I can take about a day and a half of this routine and then I am ready to go home. Barb has barely unpacked, physically or emotionally.

I need to learn how to rest better. The heart is a good example of how we should work. The heart beats HARD, then relaxes. Beats HARD, then relaxes. Beats HARD, then relaxes. The Bible says we should work hard, but then we should relax a beat. Then we can work hard again. Take five-minute naps. Take a walk around the block. I go to the museum sometimes when I'm stressed, and put my mind in neutral for a half-hour or so, or park by the lake and watch the ducks for a few minutes at lunchtime. When we are continually strained by work, in time we will break. Our bodies cannot stand the constant stress.

Resting in the Lord involves us emotionally too. Once we have done everything we feel we can do in a certain situation, we need to relax, let God do His work, and not worry. As I've mentioned before, it's not just a matter of sitting on our couch and letting God do the work. We have to DO appropriate things too.

For instance, I hate snow, and since we have a steep driveway, I've been known to worry whether it was going to snow tomorrow. I came to realize it's a bit dumb to worry about something I have no control over. But there is something I can do. When the weather forecast is for possible snow, I park my car up the hill on the street. I do what is appropriate, and then rest.

• • •

He will give eternal life to *those who patiently do the will of God*, seeking for the unseen glory and honor and eternal life that he offers. (Romans 2:7)

The first thought that comes to my mind from this passage is the problem of patiently doing God's will in a trial. Let's say you are in a job you really don't like, yet you feel it is God's will you stay where you are, rather than looking for something else. Your prayer at this point is, "Lord, teach me what You want me to learn through this trial."

On the other hand, there are times when God uses trials to move us on to something else. The only way we can tell the difference is to keep our noses in the Bible, asking God to clearly lead us. If we are undecided, then the best thing is to do nothing.

Sometimes we suffer without anyone knowing about it. This verse indicates that God is the One who gives us glory and honor, even if men don't. And on top of that, there is the bonus of eternal life. Doing the will of God patiently will result in eternal honor.

• • •

We can rejoice, too, when we run into problems and trials, for we know that they are good for us — they help us learn to be patient. And *patience develops strength of character in us*, and helps us trust God more each time we use it, until finally our hope and faith are strong and steady. (Romans 5:3) of the concepts brought up time and again in Scripture is what our attitudes should be during trials. We should rejoice. But how in the world can we rejoice when our world is collapsing around us?

We can rejoice because we trust God enough to know He has a purpose; we know what is happening to us is for our own good, and is helping us be patient. Our patience then helps build our character so we become mature in our faith.

If I had been writing the script, a Christian wouldn't have trials. We wouldn't need patience, because everything would come up roses.

The big problem is that God turned this world over to Satan. We are IN the world, but not OF the world. We are affected by cancer, war, death, disease, selfishness, and other similar things because we are still here. Someday, when we see Christ face to face, all that will be behind us. What a great day that will be!

In the meantime, we are in this sinful world and need God's strength to be patient during the hard times we experience. We need God's perspective, His big picture, in order to deal with what seems to us to be a mistake.

• • •

Be glad for all God is planning for you. *Be patient in trouble*, and prayerful always. (Romans 12:12)

I don't see a qualifying phrase in this Scripture that would indicate we are to be glad only for the "good" things. Therefore this must mean that whatever happens to us is according to God's plan, if our heart's desire is to be in the center of His will.

Sure, we can rebel and tell God to get lost. We can reject God's plan for us. We aren't robots. We have a free will to choose to follow Him or to choose not to. So I take this verse as applying to people who want to serve God. Their response should then be gladness, because they trust that God knows all about their situation, and has a plan.

When trouble comes our way, we are to be patient, letting God work out His plan. And we're to keep in touch with Him through prayer to make sure our attitudes are right.

• • •

Always be full of joy in the Lord. I say it again, rejoice!
Let everyone see that you are unselfish and considerate
in all you do. Remember that the Lord is coming soon.
Don't worry about anything; instead, pray about everything.
Tell God your needs and don't forget to thank him for his
answers. If you do this you will experience God's peace,
which is far more wonderful than the human mind can
understand. His peace will keep your thoughts and your
hearts quiet and at rest as you trust in Christ Jesus.
(Philippians 4:4-7)

There's that word *rejoice* again. As we patiently work through trials, people who watch us will be impressed by our consideration for others, even during our trial.

If we don't have patience, then we'll worry. God asks us not to worry, but to pray. The result: Experiencing God's peace, keeping us quiet and at rest.

The word *blessed* that Jesus uses in the Sermon on the Mount means "having a sense of God's approval." If you have ever had this sense, you know how delicious it is — to know you are exactly where God wants you to be, doing exactly what He wants you to do, which can include working through a trial. Even through the tears we can have a sense that God knows all about it, and has a plan, and we can smile through the tears as we trust Him to work it out.

It's a little like a new dessert. You have no idea how good it is until you taste it. You will have no idea what it means to have a sense of God's approval unless you are sold out to obedience.

And by the way, if you're bothered to see in this verse the phrase, "the Lord is coming soon," when you know it has been more than nineteen hundred years since those words were written, remember that we have to look at this from God's perspective. The view that the New Testament writers had of the future was a little like the view we get looking at mountains on the horizon — we don't see the valleys between the receding peaks. In effect, God's offer of salvation to the Gentiles was a huge valley that wasn't fully evident to these writers.

God is not slow in sending Christ back to earth. He's just being patient. And since the Bible says a thousand years is like a day to the Lord, we haven't even finished the second day, from God's viewpoint.

I think Christ will come back for His church before the close of this century, but maybe there are other valleys I can't see. My focus should be on trying to be the person God wants me to be today — and let tomorrow take care of itself.

• • •

These things that were written in the Scriptures so long ago are to teach us patience and to encourage us so that we will look forward expectantly to the time when God will conquer sin and death. May God who gives patience, steadiness, and encouragement help you to live in complete harmony with each other; each with the attitude of Christ toward the other. (Romans 15:4-5)

Here we are instructed to be patient as we look to the future coming of our Lord. God knows how anxious we are to be relieved from this world of pain, but He wants us to put the future aside and focus on today — on each other. It's fine to look forward to the rapture, but of equal importance is living in harmony with our family, our neighbors, the people we work with, our boss, the people at church, and the people at the tennis club and the union hall.

Christ is our model in this. What was His attitude? He was gentle, a good listener, patient, unconditionally loving, quick to forgive, tender, kind. Those are the same attributes we should have.

That eliminates judgmental attitudes, harshness, revenge, hatred, jumping to conclusions, impatience, and lack of forgiveness.

• • •

Love is patient and kind, never jealous or envious, never boastful or proud, never haughty or selfish or rude. Love does not demand its own way. It is not irritable or touchy. It does not hold grudges and will hardly even notice when others do it wrong. It is never glad about injustice, but rejoices whenever truth wins out. If you love someone you will be loyal to him no matter what the cost. You will always believe in him, always expect the best of him, and always stand your ground in defending him. (1 Corinthians 13:4-7)

What a beautiful picture this passage is of how God wants us to love. If we had this kind of attitude toward others, there would be no wars, no conflicts, no marriage problems, no teenage rebellion, no need for drugs and alcohol, no revenge, no hate, no backstabbing, no divorce courts, no jails. This is an ideal, of course, because we live in a world of selfishness; but we can certainly strive toward this goal.

We'll never be perfect, but we can challenge ourselves to travel as far as we can up the ladder toward the goal. We'll fail at times, but our progress is upward.

We are disappointed when we fail, but it doesn't destroy us. We ask God's forgiveness and then point our noses to the goal once again, and progress a few more steps.

If we tell ourselves, "I'm just weak in that area," or "I'm only human," or "I just can't help myself," then the direction we go is down rather than up. Even though in this life we can become only a fraction of God's ideal, we need to keep progressing toward the goal, rather than retreating in self-pity.

• • •

> We try to live in such a way that no one will ever be of-
> fended or kept back from finding the Lord by the way we
> act, so that no one can find fault with us and blame it on
> the Lord. In fact, in everything we do we try to show that
> we are true ministers of God. *We patiently endure suffering
> and hardship and trouble of every kind.* We have been beaten,
> been put in jail, faced angry mobs, worked to exhaustion,
> stayed awake through sleepless nights of watching, and
> gone without food. We have proved ourselves to be what
> we claim by our wholesome lives and by our under-
> standing of the Gospel and by our patience. (2 Corinthi-
> ans 6:3-6)

When I see the kind of things that tested the apostle Paul's
patience, it puts my piddly problems to shame. Can you
imagine how you would feel facing angry mobs, being
beaten, being jailed, or going hungry for doing right? Paul's
patient trust in God had to be deeply rooted for him to face
all this without ever once saying he'd had enough!

The first sentence in this passage tells me that we are to
live our faith in God. We can spout off all sorts of Christian
phrases and memory verses, but if people don't see biblical
principles in our lives, why will they care about what we
have to say? As author Joe Aldrich says, our non-Christian
friends need to be attracted by the MUSIC of the Gospel
before they'll hear the words.

Our lives are what God uses to win people to His Son
Jesus Christ. If we become impatient with what God is doing
in our lives, this shows we have very little trust, and the
people around us assume that God doesn't give us any more
power to endure than they have without God.

• • •

> And let us not get tired of doing what is right, for after a
> while we will reap a harvest of blessing if we *don't get
> discouraged and give up*. (Galatians 6:9)

God expects obedience from us, and if we deliberately go against what He wants us to do, we suffer the consequences and miss His blessing. God's blessing comes only when we don't give up. He will give us the strength to endure to the end.

Once again let me point out that this doesn't mean we will be perfect. It is the heart attitude that counts. If our desire is to please God in everything we do, then we'll be surprised and disappointed when we give in to temptation or fail in some other way. We will quickly ask forgiveness, and go on.

It's like losing five yards on second down. On the next play you focus on making up that lost yardage and enough more to get a first down. You don't get defeated by the yards you lost. We need to quickly put our failures behind us, and press on toward the goal.

•   •   •

So ever since we first heard about you we have kept on praying and asking God to help you understand what he wants you to do, asking him to make you wise about spiritual things, and asking that the way you live will always please the Lord and honor him, so that you will always be doing good, kind things for others, while all the time you are learning to know God better and better. We are praying, too, that you will be filled with his mighty, glorious strength, so that you can *keep going no matter what happens* — always full of the joy of the Lord. (Colossians 1:9-11)

The principles here that we've seen in other passages — making our lives pleasing to the Lord, reaching out in love, staying in His Word so we get to know Him better, taking advantage of His strength to help us keep going no matter what, all with an attitude of joy — all this is possible in our lives only if we know God through a personal trust in His Son Jesus Christ. We simply can't do them without His help.

• • •

> Since you have been chosen by God who has given you
> this new kind of life, and because of his deep love and
> concern for you, you should practice tenderhearted
> mercy and kindness to others. Don't worry about making
> a good impression on them but *be ready to suffer quietly
> and patiently.* Be gentle and ready to forgive; never hold
> grudges. Remember, the Lord forgave you, so you must
> forgive others. (Colossians 3:12-13)

Here's the same thread again: When we suffer, we need to do
it quietly and patiently.

It reminds me of Christ's words about the religious folks
who put on mourning clothes to show everyone they were
fasting. Jesus suggested that they instead put on colorful
clothes of celebration, so no one would know they were suffering. Then it would be God giving them honor, instead of
just men.

We not only need to be patient in suffering, but also quick
to forgive. This is one of the toughest things for me to do personally. I really want the other person to suffer a little too.
But God keeps bringing the person back to mind in a trou-
bling way until I really forgive him.

When I think of how much the Lord has forgiven me,
then the least I can do is forgive those who offend me. It isn't
always easy to do this — but God makes it possible.

• • •

> Dear brothers, warn those who are lazy; comfort those
> who are frightened; take tender care of those who are
> weak; and *be patient with everyone.* See that no one pays
> back evil for evil, but always try to do good to each other
> and to everyone else. Always be joyful. Always keep on
> praying. No matter what happens, always be thankful,
> for this is God's will for you who belong to Christ Jesus.
> (1 Thessalonians 5:14-18).

Here again we see the biblical threads that go with patience: caring for others, not seeking revenge, persistence in joy and prayer, and recognition that God has a plan for us.

• • •

> Again I say, don't get involved in foolish arguments which only upset people and make them angry. *God's people must not be quarrelsome; they must be gentle, patient teachers of those who are wrong.* Be humble when you are trying to teach those who are mixed up concerning the truth. For if you talk meekly and courteously to them they are more likely with God's help to turn away from their wrong ideas and believe what is true. (2 Timothy 2:23-25)

There is only one correct interpretation of biblical truth. God did not try to make His book confusing. With proper study of the context and original languages, the meaning of a passage should be quite clear.

For sure, there are a few passages where the circumstances might not be crystal clear. Most arguments about Scripture don't really affect our everyday life anyway. I think God was careful to protect the important principles so we can know clearly what He wants us to do and not to do.

All kinds of denominations, splinter groups, and cults have misinterpreted Scripture, but our attitude must be one of loving the person even if we reject his doctrine or belief. The quickest way to turn someone off is to be "holier than thou." I hate that, and I think God does too.

He doesn't want us to be argumentative. When we have the opportunity to point out an error, we should do it softly, with humble gentleness, and with dependence on God's help to set others on the right path.

• • •

Dear brothers, is your life full of difficulties and temptations? Then be happy, for *when the way is rough your patience has a chance to grow.* So let it grow, and don't try to squirm out of your problems. For when your patience is finally in full bloom, then you will be ready for anything, strong in character, full and complete. (James 1:2-4)

Here are those words again — *be happy.* And they are given once more in the context of trials and difficulties. It appears that our patience can grow only as we are faced with problems.

Our attitude in response to these problems should be one of endurance — of going THROUGH the problem rather than trying to get out of it. We short-change God's blessing when we quit.

As we grow in patience and learn to give up control, the next trial that hits us in the face won't be quite as bad, because God gives us strength to face whatever He allows or designs for our life.

WHY ME, LORD?

I DON'T LIKE PROBLEMS. I'm into pleasure and joy, not pain and suffering. There is no good reason I can think of why things can't go my way, on my time schedule, the way I want things to work out. I failed God so many times in the early days by getting upset when things blew apart.

I don't clap my hands with glee when difficult things happen now, but I do have a bigger picture — God's perspective on suffering and problems. It's like a cross-stitch. The underside is a mess — colors crisscrossing all over the place, no rhyme or reason to it. But when viewed from the top, it's a beautiful butterfly or teddy-bear or mountain scene. That's how our problems appear to God. He sees the big picture, the reason, the harmony in what we are going through. All we see is the mess underneath. We need to trust Him that He really does have a master plan for our lives. It's up to us to obey and let Him call the shots.

As I was writing this, Barb came down to the office to tell me a fuse had blown. I knew why. It was because of the crummy roof gutters. We have some workers here who are fixing them and they needed to plug their drill into the fountain outlet where the circulating motor froze this winter, next to the broken stonework someone crushed with his car, by the storm drain that is plugged with leaves. Leaves also plugged the gutters, which caused the problem in the first place or the workmen wouldn't be here.

It doesn't bother me one bit when the gutters fill up with leaves and little trees begin to grow out of them. In fact, I kinda like the effect. It makes a nice wind break, a kind of framing effect around the edge of the house. Also, if we would let the gutters get filled up once, then everything else would just drop to the ground and we wouldn't have to use our sunset years cleaning them again. Barb doesn't quite see it that way. She wants the gutters cleaned.

Barb has a real thing about leaves. We have 9,856 leafing trees around our place, and every autumn they "leaf" all over our driveway and yard. My thought — and I'm sure you'll agree it's logical — is to wait until February when all the leaves have made their way to the turf, and then rake them up. But Barb has this funny idea about raking several times during the season. In fact, as each leaf clicks and lets go of the branch and flutters to the ground with a thump, she can hear it from anywhere in the house. At that point, she wants someone to go out and rake it up — or clean it out of the gutter, thereby depriving innocent little trees of life.

Barb doesn't like moss either. We have some bricks on our patio where mosslings gather for picnics and family outings. After a few months the bricks begin to take on a green hue, as the mossling families grow in number. Barb's idea is to destroy all these innocent things, creating all sorts of trauma. Because of Barb, I go ahead and destroy them, but not without guilt pangs (I hate hurting such innocent creatures).

Now maybe you don't wrestle with leaves, or gutters, or mosslings, but I can imagine other things in your life cause you to suffer once in awhile. And we don't want to suffer — at least I don't. I want things to go smoothly so I can do all the things I WANT to do, not all the things I HAVE to do. I hate to have things happen that are out of my control, like too much rain, snow, death of a loved one, loss of a job, an earthquake, or other tragedies.

As I read the Bible, I realize suffering is part of the Christian life, even though that is not how I would have written the script. God has given Satan control in this world of sin, but God also promised to help us go through the problems that result.

Suffering is inevitable, so we might as well get used to the idea. As author and preacher Chuck Swindoll has said, once we agree that life can be difficult, it is no longer difficult.

Sometimes trials and problems are not only allowed by God, but actually DESIGNED by Him. Does that bother you? It did me for a while until I realized I learn my best lessons through pain. God is trying to mold me into the image of His Son. In this life I will never complete that process, but my goal is to be like Christ. Trials help me with my patience, self-control, peace, and faith, and help me react with strength so the people around me will be encouraged to go through their trials too.

I've been known to stretch the timing of the trials God allows or brings into my life. Let's say He has a great two week trial to check out my patience. At the end of the two weeks I'm still fighting Him, asking "Why are You doing this?" I may be worried and depressed and have lost focus. God then extends the trial another week because I haven't learned the lesson He wanted me to learn yet. If I'm still fighting Him at the end of three weeks, He extends it another week. Finally I get to the point of saying, "Lord, please teach me what You want me to learn through this trial." I learn the lesson, and He releases me from that particular problem.

Let me quickly add that even though God may be the author of trials at times, He never tempts. Satan tempts. Our own flesh tempts, but God never tempts. We can, however, change a trial into a temptation if we don't handle it right.

Sometimes our natural response to suffering and trials is

to assume that God doesn't know about them. Trials have all kinds of beneficial things for us, two of which are found in James 1:2-4.

> Dear brothers, is your life full of difficulties and temptations? Then be happy, for when the way is rough, your patience has a chance to grow. So let it grow, and don't try to squirm out of your problems. For when your patience is finally in full bloom, then you will be ready for anything, strong in character, full and complete.

These verses show that trials are "when" and not "if". They will come no matter how hard we pray or how many times we go to church. These verses also show us that trials have purpose. The sooner we accept these facts, the sooner we'll make an impact on the people around us, especially our non-Christian friends.

When nonbelievers see Christians handle their struggles and trials the same way they do, why would they need Christ in their lives? If Christianity doesn't make a difference in the way we act, who needs it? If our attitude is "Why me?" our focus is inward, not outward. We need to get on top of our circumstances, not let them get on top of us.

As I mentioned in the cross-stitch example, when we are on top of our circumstances, we can see the big picture as God sees it. But when we are under our circumstances, all we can see are the problems, the struggles, and the pain. We need to be able to thank God for our trials, assuming He has a purpose in allowing us to experience them. The only way we can do this is by keeping close to Him through His Word.

Scores of media salesmen call on me in my advertising business. I have to learn to trust them as people before I can trust what they tell me about their station or product. The better I get to know them, the more I can trust their product. That's the way our relationship with God needs to be. We have to get to know Him so well we can trust Him to have a purpose even when problems come. And the only way we can know God is by saturating ourselves in His Word.

Some of my problems result from being unable to do all the things I have planned. One day I was away from the office running an errand, and when I got back to where my car was parked on the street, it wouldn't start. I could have complained (as I sometimes do in situations like this), and asked God, "Why did You allow the car to stop working? Didn't You know I was in a hurry?" But as I've gotten more and more into His Word, I'm able to give the situation to God, as I did this time. I was grateful the car had stopped working while it was parked rather than when I was driving on the freeway or on a bridge. I was glad it happened on an afternoon when I had no emergency meetings or crisis appointments. As it was, I put some money in the meter and walked back to the office, which was only a few blocks away. I was thanking God for the situation, assuming that whatever He had planned was okay with me.

Later that afternoon I had the car towed home, and for the rest of the week I drove a small pickup we use for the business. I'm just a farm boy anyway, so driving the truck was no big deal. In fact it was fun. Two days later, I noticed I had a lunch scheduled with a brand-new Christian who repaired appliances for a living. I drove to his shop, went inside, and instantly realized why God had stopped my car. The guy would have been very uncomfortable riding in a luxury car in his work clothes and probably would not have been able to relate to me very well. But he was at home in a truck, since he drove one every day. We had a fantastic lunch, sharing Christ with each other, building up each other, having a great time.

When I see Christ face to face, I'm going to ask Him, "Did You really make my car stop so I could drive the truck to see my friend?" He may say, "No, it was just your PCV valve," but I suspect He will say, "Yes, you see, before the foundation of the world We knew your friend would be threatened by a big car until he got to know you, so We just decided to stop your car for a while and let you drive the truck."

From God's viewpoint, my inconvenience was a thou-

sand times less important than having lunch with my friend.
God is just that practical. I thank Him so much for a beautiful
verse which says,

> We can make our plans, but the final outcome is in God's
> hands. (Proverbs 16:1)

Does that concept bother you? I'm not a robot. My every
step is not dictated by God. I can choose to follow His plan
for my life. I just feel it makes a lot of sense for me to fit into
His plans because He sees the future perfectly. I've failed too
many times when I've tried to do things on my own.

We once had someone working for us whom we discovered to be dishonest. I had every reason to march into the
office, ask the person to leave, and require restitution for the
wrongs done. But I didn't have peace about doing that. So I
prayed, "Lord, I know You want so-and-so to leave, and so
do I, but I'll leave the timing up to You." Several weeks went
by without a solution. So I took the problem back from God
and wrestled with it on my own. I could hardly be around
that person, because I was so suspicious and uneasy and
worried.

Then once again I prayed, "Lord, I know You want so-
and-so to leave, but it's Your problem now." This went on for
several months until one day in desperation I prayed something like, "It's a real mystery why You haven't caused this
person to leave. Could it be you want this person to stay? If
so, please help me to accept Your will in this matter. I really
do want to please You, not myself." In two weeks the person
was gone. There was no confrontation, no bad feelings. When
I completely turned it over to God, He answered in His own
time, which was perfect.

I know that sometimes we need to confront dishonest or
disloyal people, but in this case I feel God was trying to teach
me how to let go of all the strings and be patient.

Paul wrote to the Corinthians about another reason for
suffering and trials besides those that mature us and build
our character or teach us patience:

What a wonderful God we have — he is the Father of our
Lord Jesus Christ, the source of every mercy, and the one
who so wonderfully comforts and strengthens us in our
hardships and trials. And why does he do this? So that
when others are troubled, needing our sympathy and en-
couragement, we can pass on to them this same help and com-
fort God has given us. You can be sure that the more we
undergo sufferings for Christ, the more he will shower us
with his comfort and encouragement. (2 Corinthians 1:3-
5)

Time after time, as Barb and I take troubled couples out
to dinner and begin sharing some of the problems we've had
in our marriage, the other couple will say something like,
"That happened to us last week. What do we do about it?"
Then we can relate some of the practical lessons we've
learned through various situations and from Scripture, and
offer them the same comfort God gave us. The longer I live,
the more I can see God bringing into our lives people who
can benefit from the lessons we have learned by going
THROUGH our problems, instead of trying to get out of
them.

God uses difficulties to make us better and more useful to
others. We all want to be used for Christ's highest purposes,
but we have to be the right kind of dish or vessel. Chuck
Swindoll tells of some archaeological digs in Greece in which
they found clay pots with the Greek word *dokimas* stamped
on the bottom. The word means "approved through the fire,"
meaning that this particular pot had been through the kiln
and didn't crack under the heat. People knew they could put
their best olive oil or wine in the pot and it wouldn't break.

What a beautiful picture of what we should be for God —
a vessel uncracked, proven through the fires of struggle and
trial, fit for God's best purposes. God doesn't put us through
the fire to see when we'll crack. He puts us there to temper us
and make us strong so we will be ready for anyone and anything that might come along.

As we deal with struggles and problems, we may not know at the time why they happen to us. However, God often shows us the reason for a particular trial AFTER we have gone through it. When we face difficulties, our natural tendency is to give up and quit, but God's Word says just the opposite. Here's one of my favorite passages concerning problems:

> We are pressed on every side by troubles, but not crushed and broken. We are perplexed because we don't know why things happen as they do, but we don't give up and quit. We are hunted down, but God never abandons us. We get knocked down, but we get up again and keep going. These bodies of ours are constantly facing death just as Jesus did; so it is clear to all that it is only the living Christ within who keeps us safe. (2 Corinthians 4:8-10)

The first part of this verse reminds me of the movie *Star Wars*. In one scene the good guys were trapped in a big garbage crusher and the four sides were closing in on them. I've been in situations where I felt like that. Everything was closing in on me. It was only through God's strength that I survived.

In this passage I also like the picture of being knocked down but getting up again. It reminds me of those furry dolls at the fair with lead in their feet. They just pop right back up when they're knocked down. Once in a while we get knocked down too. Then what do we do?

> So take a new grip with your tired hands, stand firm on your shaky legs, and mark out a straight, smooth path for your feet so that those who follow you, though weak and lame, will not fall and hurt themselves, but become strong. (Hebrews 12:12-13)

One of my chores on the farm was bringing in the milk buckets from the barn. They were running over with fresh milk, and quite heavy. Once in a while I would have to stop

and get a new grip on the handle. Though it seems this passage in Hebrews is mostly about getting up after God has
had to discipline us, I think we can use the same principle
with suffering and trials. When they knock us down we can
get up again. We don't have to stay down. In fact, if we stay
defeated it proves we really don't have much of God's
strength in us after all.

One day I received a call from a young wife going
through financial problems brought on by her husband's
mistakes. "When will it end?" she asked. "I can't stand any
more. I want it to be over. Why is this happening to me?" I
told her that I have searched the Scriptures and can't find any
promises that our problems will ever end until Christ returns
or we die. But I do know trials help us grow — and what's so
bad about growing? It hurts, but who has our best in mind?
God. And what has He promised? To see us through our
problems. He seeks results with eternal purposes, to prepare
for both a better life on earth, and a fantastic life in heaven,
and we need to keep an eternal perspective. The years He
gives us down here won't last very long. The book of James
calls life a "vapor," and the older I get the more vaporized
life becomes.

In a shop class in high school, we made chisels. We put
them into the fire to temper and harden them so they would
be prepared for the hammer blows later. In the same way,
God puts us through the furnace of adversity.

Part of this tempering process involves being a servant. A
servant is one who does the will of the master, no matter
what he is asked to do. God may be saying, "I want you to
grow through this sickness. I have another person who will
come into your life later who will need the same comfort I
am giving you now." As God's servants, we need to do the
things He wants us to do — and do them *when* He wants,
how He wants, and *where* He wants, even if it causes us suffering.

One of the best ways to respond to a trial or suffering is
to remember all the ways God has helped us in the past — to
remember all the prayers He has answered with a "Yes."

Once in a while I hear a person say, "God didn't answer my prayer." Sure He did. His answer was "Wait" or "No," which are the hardest answers for us to hear. We can get all bent out of shape when we don't get a yes, because we don't see the big picture — but we can trust that God's timing is perfect.

The key to handling suffering and trials is to see them from God's perspective. We need to look through the trial, beyond the trial, and above the trial. We need to get on top of our circumstances rather than being buried under the pile. So often we let trials make us bitter, when God's purpose is to make us better. When I come to a trial I want relief, but God wants my maturity. Contentment depends on our focus, not on the trial itself. If we are focusing on God and what He is trying to do through our lives, we can endure the suffering. If we are focusing on our circumstances, we become bitter, angry, and defeated.

Our dogs Molly and Muffit are good examples. They spend most of their time in the backyard or in the house or in the car, but once in a while we put a leash on them and go for a walk. They pull and choke and strain and cough and struggle. They would have a much happier walk if they would just relax and work within the "trial." That's a picture of us. We choke and struggle and strain against the trial, and have a miserable time. When we assume God is working for our best, and we relax and try to fit into His plans, things go much smoother for us.

A TRAGIC GAP—We need to be honest about our hurts. A pastor once asked me to what I attributed the growth of a class Barb and I taught. I told him we tried to stay close to the Word and also tried to be vulnerable and share our present hurts and struggles. He said he had been taught in seminary to leave a little gulf between the pulpit and the first pew—in other words, to not be vulnerable. I responded, "That's one reason it took God thirty-eight years to get my attention and convince me that Christ and the Bible could affect my life. I had no idea my teachers and pastors had struggles too."

When our focus is to shorten the test or change the course to make it more comfortable, we often will short-change God's plan to build our patience and our character. If we get out of the trial, we don't learn the lessons He has for us to mold us more into the image of His Son. Satan's greatest effort is not to get us to hate God, but to get us to forget His reality when we are under a trial.

Someone has said (and I love this), "God does not make life easy. He just makes it possible!" Thank You, Lord, for Your unspeakable gift of helping us face the trials of life.

13

THE TICKET
I DESERVE

THERE'S ANOTHER REASON FOR SUFFERING, and we don't like to talk about it: Sometimes we suffer for doing wrong. If I go seventy miles an hour on the freeway and get a ticket, I deserve the ticket. It surely doesn't make much sense for me to grouse around, mumbling against God for bringing this "suffering" into my life. I simply have to pay the consequences for my sin, then get up and go on.

I know quite a few people who are suffering for the wrongs they have done, but are getting impatient with God. It's almost as if they want God to start over, to erase the consequences of their sins. We should pick up and go on after we blow it and not look back, after asking for forgiveness from God (and from any people involved). This does not mean the consequence of adultery, divorce, stealing, or lying will go away automatically when we get our behavior straightened out. There is a price to pay for sin, and the best thing we can do is be patient and let God work out His will in the situation.

We sin because we are tempted to sin, and because we don't resist the temptation. God does not let us be tempted beyond what we are able to stand. However, He doesn't "set us up" for failure either. When Miss Temptation knocks on the door of our mind, we have two alternatives: Ask her in, or shut her out. If we ask her to come on in so we can think about the situation for a while, we are saying, "Don't call me, God. I'll call you" — since God takes a hike when we give in to temptation, and leaves us on our own. We have to shut the door on temptation immediately.

Satan knows what makes us tick and where we have weaknesses. If we have a tendency to steal, he'll make sure we have plenty of opportunities to take what isn't ours without anyone ever knowing. If we struggle with lust, he'll make sure we see all kinds of TV shows, movies, and magazines to help feed this weakness and turn our thoughts into actions.

Nobody fishes with a screwdriver tied to a string. If we did, the fish would hurt themselves laughing. To catch fish we put a wiggly, fat, juicy worm on the end of the line and if they're hungry, pretty soon we've got 'em. That's what Satan does to us. He doesn't waste his time in the areas of our strengths. His favorite lures are the things we have a weakness for, and he begins his subtle work in our minds. If *Playboy*, *Showtime*, and R and X-rated videos are our daily mind food, our minds will be sensual. But if the Bible is our daily food, our minds will be spiritual. There will still be an occasional battle, but if we're properly nourished, God can help us win. As someone has said, a dusty Bible results in a dirty life.

So what are we supposed to do when confronted by temptation? Joseph in the Old Testament gave us a clue. He had been put in charge of the prime minister's entire estate — everything except the prime minister's wife. Over a period of time she made passes at Joseph, and one day when the boss was out of town and all the servants were in the field, she made one more pass at him. Do you know what he did? He RAN! Why would he do that, when it was the perfect situation and no one would know? Because God would know, so Joseph took off rather than commit a sin against the prime minister and against God.

If you do not have a sensual problem you wonder what's so hard about running away from a temptation like this. But if you do have struggles in this area you know EXACTLY what Joseph was facing, and the strength he showed by doing the right thing. We need models like this to encourage us to run from the temptations Satan puts in our path.

I once visited an aluminum plant. I watched the heated metal being pushed through dies to come out shaped as gutters, molding, angles, or rods. As Christians, God heats us up and pushes us through the die of struggles and problems in order to shape us into what He wants us to be. How much pressure and heat is needed to push us through God's machine to make us like Christ? As with the metal, just enough to overcome the natural resistance of the material being molded. What this says to me is the more we fight or resist, the more pressure and heat God has to exert in order to mold us into the image of Christ.

We don't have to dwell on past problems and mistakes. We need to take care of today and press on toward the future.

> He has given you all of the present and all of the future. (1 Corinthians 3:22)

God forgets our sins...why can't we? We should learn to live as Paul did —

> Forgetting the past and looking forward to what lies ahead... (Philippians 3:13)

Punishment looks to the past; discipline looks to the future. That's important to keep in mind. It helps us see problems from God's perspective:

> These troubles and sufferings of ours are, after all, quite small and won't last very long. Yet this short time of distress will result in God's richest blessing upon us forever and ever! (2 Corinthians 4:17)

I look at myself as a channel, wanting to be clean and pure so God's love can flow through me to other people. If I'm contaminated with anger, bitterness, lust, or jealousy, then I block God's love. And when I'm contaminated like that, I can't have the effect in other people's lives that God wants me to have.

14

A WORKOUT

WE CAN BE JOYFUL through the tears of trials. As our patience develops and our strength grows, we learn to trust God more. We know God loves us and will not allow anything to come into our lives that is not in our best interest. He goes through the problem with us, because the Holy Spirit is right there inside us, filling our hearts with the knowledge of God's love.

But we can't trust someone we don't know. How can we trust God with problems if we don't know Him?

And how can we know Him without getting into the Bible on a regular basis?

And how can we get into the Bible on a regular basis without working at it?

Barb and I know a number of professional athletes here in Seattle and around the country. We see how hard they work before the cheers begin. They punish their bodies by making them do things they don't want to do, like running, lifting weights, doing push-ups, working out on exercise equipment, and then running some more.

For some reason the world really doesn't expect to see Christians work hard. Non-Christians tend to see Christians as sissies, wimps, or pushovers. But Paul wrote:

> I'm not just shadow-boxing or playing around. Like an athlete I punish my body, treating it roughly, training it to do what it should, not what it wants to. Otherwise I fear that after enlisting others for the race, I myself might be declared unfit and ordered to stand aside." (1 Corinthians 9:26-27)

A Christian should run his or her race to win, to gain first place in business or athletics, to be the best homemaker possible, the best neighbor, the best church member, the best pastor, the best truck driver, the best advertising agency person. We should run with purpose, setting goals, eyeing the mark, denying self, and being the best Christian we can possibly be.

Part of our "exercise" includes programming our minds to act in the right way automatically. A football coach wants to have his players get to a point where they don't have to think when they go to make a block or set up a defense. He wants them to react instinctively. That's the way God wants us to act too. If we pre-program ourselves with the Word, then we can act the right way when faced with a temptation, trial, surprise, or someone cutting us off on the freeway. God wants us to act instinctively so we can react His way, rather than reacting in our natural way.

Having that kind of response takes practice — disciplined training. God gives us His grace and spiritual power to enable us to change, but we still must do our part.

Time is too short to play games in the Christian life. We can't have one foot on the dock and one foot on the ship and expect to go anywhere. As I've heard Chuck Swindoll say, some of us have too much of the world to be comfortable with Christ, and too much of Christ to be comfortable in the world.

I used to work with a man who acted and sounded like a Christian when he was with Christians, but when he was with non-Christians he acted and sounded just like one of them. The non-Christians in his life knew he should not be involved in some of the things he was doing, yet I suppose it gave them some comfort to drag him down a bit. The Christians in his life knew he was a fake because his walk didn't match his talk. He was basically a lazy Christian.

We can't be like that if we mean business about transforming our thoughts and actions, knowing the Bible, and knowing and trusting God. Laziness won't cut it.

It takes effort — but amazingly enough, once we truly want to know and trust God, and are committed to working hard at learning what the Bible says about Him, He rewards us with rich insights and blessings far beyond what our attempts deserve.

He's that kind of God!

15

IT'S A SAFE TRIP—
SO WHY WORRY?

I USED TO TAKE TIM AND BEV to the shopping mall to "drive" around the empty parking lot. They would sit on my lap and we would drive all over the place. Sometimes on the back roads I would let them hold the wheel. But they weren't really driving — I was, though they didn't seem to notice I had my hands on the wheel.

In the same way the Holy Spirit has His hand on the steering wheel as we "drive" our lives. Because we are not robots, we can, if we choose, force His hands off the controls; but then we take responsibility for the failures that follow. For me, it's a real comfort to know He is driving, and I'm just along for the ride. I like it that way.

But I sometimes resist the Holy Spirit by worrying about the road ahead. I find myself asking, "What if...?" What if I lose one of my clients? What if I get cancer? What if it snows? What if one of our children or grandchildren is kidnapped? What if our home burns down? What if the sun burns out? (Some of our worry is just that silly when we look at it in perspective; someone has estimated that ninety-five percent of the things we worry about never happen.) Worry, according to Bill Gothard, can be defined as accepting responsibility for something God never intended us to carry. I've been known to worry about whether it's going to rain on our picnic next week. Since I can't control the weather, isn't that a little dumb?

The root meaning of the word translated as "worry" in Scripture is a "divided mind." We can't sleep at night sometimes worrying about the events of the next day. What if we have a flat tire? What if he rejects me? What if I fail? It is said that half of all hospital patients are there because of worry, stress, anger, or bitterness. Worry takes a terrible toll on our bodies. It can cause heart trouble, high blood pressure, asthma, rheumatism, ulcers, colds, thyroid problems, arthritis, migraine headaches, indigestion, nausea, constipation, colitis, dizziness, fatigue, insomnia, allergies, and even paralysis. Of course, if you have some of these illnesses it could be for other reasons than worry. But it would be good to take an inventory to see just how much worry you are carrying around.

Worry is contagious too. Unless you're married to one, stay away from worriers. They will drag you down. Worry is a sin, because it calls God a liar. Yet it is the most natural human response to struggles and trials.

More important than anything I could say about worry is what God has told us:

Who then can ever keep Christ's love from us? When we have trouble or calamity, when we are hunted down or destroyed, is it because he doesn't love us anymore? And if we are hungry, or penniless, or in danger, or threatened with death, has God deserted us? No, for the Scriptures tell us that for his sake we must be ready to face death at every moment of the day — we are like sheep awaiting slaughter; but despite all this, overwhelming victory is ours through Christ who loved us enough to die for us. For I am convinced that nothing can ever separate us from his love. Death can't, and life can't. The angels won't, and all the powers of hell itself cannot keep God's love away. Our fears for today, our worries about tomorrow, or where we are — high above the sky, or in the deepest ocean — nothing will ever be able to separate us from the love of God demonstrated by our Lord Jesus Christ when he died for us. (Romans 8:35-39)

It is comforting to know that no matter where we are, nothing can put a wall between us and God's love. Though it's natural for us to run away from trials, God wants us to look not for a way OUT of our problems, but for a way THROUGH them. He has never promised the absence of trials, but He has promised His supernatural help as we endure them.

16

LIFE IN THE PITS

I'VE BEEN WORKING SO HARD at the office that I'm getting bitter and resentful. I have to keep our advertising business healthy in order to pay for the various ministries God has given us. I have chosen to keep the staff small and try to do much of the client contact personally. All I really have to sell is me, and I want to serve my customers so well they won't even consider looking for another agency. I do a lot of things free to show them I can give as well as receive in business.

Staying so close to the business, however, means I have to be involved in much more detail than I might if I delegated the client contact to an employee. When my client wants to know why we're paying a premium for drive time in Prosser when the city is only two miles wide, I like to be able to give him an instant answer as often as possible. But on the other hand, I understand Albert Einstein said he remembered only those things he couldn't look up, so I just make sure I am conversant with the various resource materials we have available.

Balancing business and ministry takes on-going fine tuning. Keeping a healthy business pays for our ministries, so my clients come first and deserve my close attention. I work hard at my secular work and make that a high priority. On the other hand, the things I do here on earth will only last for a time, and there are hundreds of opportunities to affect people for eternity, so it's a constant battle of priorities.

I suppose it would be nice to be free to minister full time someday, so once in a while at one of my regular business sessions with the Lord, I'll suggest He find me a nice little gold mine close to the house, or maybe in the basement, where I could go and chip off what I need that month to live. Then I'd be able to spend my time having counseling breakfasts, lunches, and dinners, writing books, and loving my Christian and non-Christian friends full-time.

I imagine the Lord thinks about this for a few minutes and then reminds me that some of the people I want to relate to wouldn't give me the time of day if they didn't know I experienced the same pressures they did — profit-and-loss statements, employee turnover, time pressures, pension plans, overhead growth, etc. There's a terrible disadvantage in being in full-time ministry. People think you have it made and no longer experience the day-to-day struggles they have. They put you on a pedestal and then look around for a "normal" person with whom they can share their lives.

After the Lord once again reminds me why I am in business and not in full-time ministry, I return to the work at hand and once again put my nose into the day-to-day details. Meanwhile I squeeze in early breakfasts, long lunches, and late phone conversations with the people I feel God has asked me to love for Him. As the problems and challenges of the business begin to mount and more and more people come into my life to love for Christ, the time pressures become almost unbearable. It gets so bad sometimes I resent the next person who needs just a few minutes of my time, or a "simple" slide presentation for his church, or some financial advice, or employment counseling, or help to find God's will in some area. I know God doesn't want me to be bitter, resentful, and burned out, so I start cutting back on some good things that maybe aren't the BEST things for me at that point in time.

When I am buried up to my eyes in projects, a comforting thought is to reflect on what Christ said at the end of His ministry: "It is finished." His job was accomplished, even though there were still lepers, blind people, and other hurting folks all around Him. This suggests to me that I should be careful with my priorities to make sure I am working on the most important thing at any given moment. If there are some projects I don't get done, that's really God's problem. He will either impress on me to find the time to get them done or give someone else the blessing. When I get all tied up in knots, I really don't do a good job at anything.

A few months ago, as my anger, frustration, and bitterness were increasing daily, there came a Saturday when I had no immediate deadlines and only one counseling appointment. I was relishing the thought of puttering around my workshop or playing some tennis or reading a book, or perhaps doing some of the 119 projects I hadn't been able to get to.

That day the sun came out, brighter than usual for Seattle. After breakfast, my sweet wife Barb approached me with some projects to do. We had invited some people over for a barbecue, and I was to bring up the tables, put chlorine in the pool, lay out the pickle-ball court, prepare the barbecue, clean off my desks, pick up junk in the basement, sweep out the garage, and a few other things on her list. No problem.

Then Barb threw in the ringer. She also wanted the cherries picked from a tree in our backyard. For eleven of the twelve years we have lived in our present home, the squirrels have eaten every cherry before we have had a chance to get out and pick them. (They even crawl along the branches upside down to get the last ones.) As far as I'm concerned, those cherries were to feed God's furry little friends and we were meant to buy what we need at Safeway, rather than condemning those creatures to a long, cold winter without proper nutrition. There's a Scripture on this subject:

A good man is concerned for the welfare of his animals.
(Proverbs 12:10)

But this year not a squirrel was in sight (they must have
been asleep or on vacation), and the tree was loaded with lus-
cious, red, fat, ripe, juicy cherries, all crying out to Barb,
"Pick us!"

I couldn't believe I was being asked to sacrifice my Saturday to pick fruit that Barb could buy for forty-nine cents a
pound. (Where are you, you dim-witted squirrels?) But I got
the dumb ladder and the stupid bucket on a wire that hangs
on my belt, and climbed this ridiculous tree to pick some idi-
otic cherries that seemed to be splitting their seams laughing
at me.

I can't remember when I've been so upset. It ruined my
entire day and part of the next one, too. I could hardly speak
to anyone, especially Barb. I hated everything that came into
my path. To top it off, she asked me to wash the umbrella
over the picnic table. I doubted whether the people coming
over would even notice we had an umbrella, let alone
whether it was dirty. Who cares?

Barb does. So after I got done picking the cherries, I
rigged up the power nozzle my daughter gave me for my
birthday, only to find out the umbrella was in danger of
being torn to shreds by the power of the stream. I had to
scrub it by hand!

Then I had to clean the filter on the swimming pool. Our
filter has microscopic holes in its little screen, which seem to
get plugged when extra large atoms and neutrons go
through. I had earlier tried to convince Barb that cleaning the
filter was a complicated job way over my head (hoping to re-
mind her of the times I put the plastic things in the wrong
place in the dishwasher, or used fourteen clean diapers to
change one dirty one until Barb would finally say "Let me do
it," and then I could go to my shop or read). But this time the
jig was up. She taught me how to clean the filter, and it was
too simple to make her think I didn't understand.

The world was in chaos and what was I doing about it? Picking cherries, scrubbing umbrellas, and cleaning filters. I wondered how long God was going to stand for such poor stewardship on my part.

It was a fitting end to a whole week of anger-producing frustration at work. Two of my employees had traffic accidents, the copy machine and typewriter broke down, and I couldn't find essential films and tapes. Saturday was the last straw.

Then I realized what was the matter. I had agreed months ago to speak at our church on Sunday evening and the topic I had chosen was "Anger." The Lord was making me live what I was going to teach. He was intending to speak through my experiences to make them real to the people who would hear my message.

When I began my study, I first went to *Strong's Concordance* to see if anger was ever mentioned in the Bible. I found three entire columns of Scripture references. Many of them were about God's anger, such as Exodus 4:10-14.

> But Moses pleaded, "O Lord, I'm just not a good speaker. I never have been, and I'm not now, even after you have spoken to me, for I have a speech impediment." "Who makes mouths?" Jehovah asked him. "Isn't it I, the Lord? Who makes a man so that he can speak or not speak, see or not see, hear or not hear? Now go ahead and do as I tell you, for I will help you to speak well, and I will tell you what to say." But Moses said, "Lord, please! Send someone else." Then the Lord became angry.

I can just feel God's anger in this passage. He had given Moses all the gifts and talents he needed to do God's work, but he still had no self-confidence and wanted God to "send someone else." God got angry with Moses — and I'm afraid He is disappointed with me, too, when I forget that He is in control, not me.

Jesus also expressed anger:

While in Capernaum Jesus went over to the synagogue again, and noticed a man there with a deformed hand. Since it was the Sabbath, Jesus' enemies watched him closely. Would he heal the man's hand? If he did, they planned to arrest him! Jesus asked the man to come and stand in front of the congregation. Then turning to his enemies, he asked, "Is it all right to do kind deeds on Sabbath days? Or is this a day for doing harm? Is it a day to save lives or to destroy them?" But they wouldn't answer him. Looking around at them angrily, for he was deeply disturbed by their indifference to human need, he said to the man, "Reach out your hand." He did, and instantly his hand was healed! (Mark 3:1-5)

The religious leaders of Jesus' day were most often on the receiving end of His anger. But unlike Christ's anger, mine is not righteous. Mine is self-centered. Paul said we judge in others those weaknesses we find in ourselves. I dislike people who are critical, intolerant, unloving, and hold grudges, but I have the same tendencies.

When Jesus Christ went into the temple to confront the buyers and sellers, He did not say, "Guys, at your convenience, and if it meets your approval, would you please leave the temple?" He threw them out on their cash registers, with anger boiling inside Him as He saw His Father's house being used as a marketplace. But He did not sin with His anger, and I do. Nevertheless it helps to know He experienced the same feelings of frustration and anger I have. He understands me when I get angry. He experienced all the temptations and pressures I experience, but did not sin — what a model to pattern our lives after!

Just what is this anger, this rage that sometimes tears us apart and makes us explode, hurting the ones we love?

Anger is an emotion caused by the frustration of our goals and desires. It can be brought on by people, situations, or things.

I recently tried to remove some masking tape from our driveway. It had been placed there to mark out a court for playing pickle-ball. The sun and cars had pushed the tape into the crevices of the cement, and now I had to take it up in little pieces. I wanted the tape to come up in one large strip so I could spend thirty seconds at the most getting rid of it, and then get back to the football game I was missing.

I get angry when I can't find tools or sports equipment that I know I had right here a minute ago. I can see it in my mind: Someone must have moved whatever it is I've lost, just to see me squirm. Once in a great while — it happened once on May 17, 1956, and again on December 14, 1964 — I misplaced something and forgot where I put it. But those are the only two times I can remember when it was my fault. Most of the time, Satan or one of the members of my family moves whatever it is I'm looking for, and it drives me out of my mind.

In our other home we used to have what I called the Bermuda Triangle. It was our dining-room table. What is a dining-room table for? To leave things on, right? You can eat on it too, but it is placed near the front door purposely so you can leave stuff on it when you come home from work or play. For some reason, Barb thought it should never have anything on it — ever! When the kids or I would put something down on the table, it would disappear, never to be seen again, just like the ships and planes in the real Bermuda Triangle. Poof! Not even any ashes. We used to have four kids, but one of them sat on the table. Hasn't been seen since. That used to irritate me, not being able to find something I had left there. Now I have victory over that. We moved, and our present dining room table is three miles from the front door.

Anger is no stranger to me. When you think about it, I guess we were born angry. After nine beautiful months in that warm nest with every one of our needs being met, all of a sudden we experience cold air, a slap on the bottom, and a bunch of strangers standing around with video cameras.

In the book *Facing Anger* by Norman Rohrer and Philip Sutherland (Augsburg, 1981), I learned there are several basic reasons for anger. One is the desire to feel powerful. We feel weak if our behavior is determined by other people, so we become angry to restore our sense of power. The person who feels powerful doesn't need anger.

Helplessness makes us angry. People may feel angry when a person close to them dies, even becoming angry at the dead person. If our home is destroyed by a fire or flood, or a burglar cleans out all the valuables, or an accident leaves a family member hospitalized, we feel helpless. We have no power over the event, which makes us angry.

Having too many things to do in too little time makes us angry. I've always been proud that I could get a lot done, even though this pressure makes me angry at times when I get into a time squeeze. I even did six things at once recently: I dubbed a tape, worked on a slide presentation, put a record on a cassette, filled the fountain, flushed the car radiator, and ran some audio copies on my little copy machine. After I finished that record-breaking accomplishment, I rushed upstairs to share this triumph with Barb. She wasn't the least bit impressed.

The book *Type A Behavior and Your Heart* (Friedman and Rosenman, Knopf, 1974), indicated to me that Type A people — who are on the go, make impossible deadlines for themselves, hate red lights, have lots of stress, and can't relax — are more prone to heart attacks than Type B people, who relax and don't mind traffic signals and do only one thing at

> **STRENGTH UNDER CONTROL**—The world equated meekness with weakness, but the biblical concept of meekness is strength under control, and God wants to build this into His people. It's easy to pop some guy in the nose because he strikes at you. Only with God's help can we answer back softly or walk away from the confrontation. On the other hand, it takes God's help to stay in a marriage and work hard at making it what it should be, when we'd rather walk away.

a time. Barb said I wasn't supposed to glory in my being a Type A. I was supposed to try to be a Type B. Who wants to be a Type B for goodness' sake? We'd still be riding in covered wagons if some of the Type A's in our history hadn't wanted to go a little faster.

I really get angry when I'm late, which is often caused by trying to do too much at the last minute, or having too many people demanding my time. Anger is not actually produced by a situation so much as it is our interpretation of the situation. For instance, Barb feels red lights are ordained by God to bring order into our lives, while I feel red lights are direct tools of Satan to disrupt my schedule.

Another cause of anger is our desire to be self-sufficient. The toddler wants to put on his own socks. The teenager wants to fix the car. The young wife struggles to sew a dress. When we fail at tasks like these, we become angry and frustrated. We want to be in control, and this causes some of us, especially men, to avoid seeing doctors or counselors. We want to do it ourselves, and when we lose control, we get angry.

As a general rule, I would much rather go to a restaurant than to someone's home for dinner. In someone's home, I'm not in control as far as the food I'm served. They want to put on the dog, so they have cream of broccolisoufflevichysoise or some other foreign dish like carrots or spinach.

Trying to be self-sufficient hits our home life too, as we fathers and husbands try to be in control of our wives and kids. It's hard for a man to say, "I'm sorry," or "Please forgive me." So we hide the problem under the rug and bluster around until we get the upper hand. The family then sees us as insensitive and uncaring.

One of the most common causes of anger in marriage centers on differences in communication style. One partner is "nonexpressive," and the other "expressive." (Barb and I have gone into detail on this in our book *INCOMPATIBILITY: Grounds for a Great Marriage!*) When a conflict arises, the expressive person wants to talk about it right now and be friends again, while the nonexpressive NEVER wants to talk about it.

Nonexpressives like me often don't know why we are angry, or why we said something that hurt the other person. When I would tell that to Barb, she thought I must be either lying or trying to get her off my back. But I wasn't. I just couldn't put words to my feelings instantly like she could. The expressive partner needs to give the nonexpressive time to get in touch with his feelings, and the nonexpressive needs to give the expressive hope that they can talk about it some-time soon. And here's the subtle part. The expressive must create a crisis to get the nonexpressive thinking. I know this takes a lot of energy, and expressives would like to get the conflict over quickly and be friends again, but that's just the way it is.

We were driving to church one Sunday and some little doll in her Porsche was about two coats of paint off my back bumper going forty miles an hour. That drives me nuts, so I mentioned a few words I had learned on the farm working with horses. Barb was shocked, but didn't say anything. I hardly realized she even noticed.

In the next few days Barb got cooler and cooler, but said nothing. I noticed the frostbite on my fingers when I touched her, but I didn't say anything either. I wasn't sure what I had done to make her freeze up. Finally the incident with the Porsche came up and we talked about it. She wanted to know if I was living a secret life. She hadn't heard that type of lan-guage from me very often. I had asked God to forgive me, but didn't realize Barb was involved too.

After expressives create the crisis, they have to allow their nonexpressive partners enough time to get in touch with their feelings. Then the couple needs to make a date to talk about the situation.

When nonexpressives finally begin to let out their feel-ings, their expressive mate needs to LISTEN, not interrupt or advise. If your expressive mate can't keep quiet, you may want to make up a set of cue cards with words that don't occur to the expressive during a conflict. Hold the cards up high so they can be easily seen, and have your partner read the words:

What else do you feel?
Tell me more about that.
My, that's interesting.

These words usually aren't even in the expressive's vocabulary during a conflict. But when expressives evaluate too quickly, they get exactly what they don't want from the nonexpressive — anger or silence. The nonexpressive is SO FRUSTRATED at not being able to fully communicate feelings that he or she retreats behind a wall of silent anger at the first possible moment.

A practical way to solve this is with a concept called "Quick Listening." Person A talks about his or her feelings, without being interrupted. Person B then reflects back A's

---

AUTHENTICATING EMOTIONS—A small boy visiting our home fell off the front porch. It was only a foot off the ground, but he thought he was dying and began to cry. Barb said, "That really hurt, didn't it?" He immediately stopped crying, agreed with her that it hurt, and went off to play. He just needed someone to authenticate his feelings.

We men have to do the same thing for our wives. We need to mirror back their feelings in our words. Some men are very sensitive, but most of us have problems expressing our feelings or talking with other people who get emotional. We want to discuss things man-to-man, clinical, no tears, no raised voices. It's almost impossible for our wives to do this. God gave most of them the skill of sharing their emotions, both negative and positive. Men need to be taught how to do this. We appear sometimes to be indifferent beasts, but in reality we just have never been taught how to communicate well at the height of emotion.

---

statements until A agrees that this is exactly what was meant.

Then Person B talks and A reflects back B's statements. When was the last time you got all your feelings out to your mate without being interrupted? If it was recently, you are rare indeed.

The first time Barb and I did this she said, "Keep it short!" We laugh, of course, because she wants to get on with it and be friends again, and I talk and think slowly and have trouble putting my feelings into words.

My guess is that about ninety percent of marriage conflicts could be solved if each partner heard everything the other wanted to say. When the nonexpressive retreats behind anger, everything shuts down above the chin. The blood goes to the muscles and inner organs, and the brain does not get its share during this time of rage. Angry people are not thinking clearly. They say things they don't mean. They strike out.

You cannot reason with an angry person. Don't even try. Wait until he or she cools down to begin a logical conversation. Try to mirror back the anger if you can, so the other person can get rid of if rather than stuff it.

There's a Bible verse relating to anger that has been misinterpreted in my opinion:

> If you are angry, don't sin by nursing your grudge. Don't let the sun go down with you still angry — get over it quickly, for when you are angry you give a mighty foothold to the devil. (Ephesians 4:26-27)

Judging from the rest of Scripture, God is fair with His rules, so I have to think He knows how hard it is for us nonexpressives to get in touch with our feelings. If it takes us a day or two to figure out why we are angry and to put words to our feelings, it doesn't seem logical that He would zap us with lightning before we had a chance to do that. I don't think He means for us to stay up for forty-eight hours until we can solve the problem and be friends again. I think God allows a couple to AGREE before the sun goes down to solve the problem. The expressive can agree to give the nonexpressive time to get in touch with his or her feelings, and the nonexpressive can agree to make a date to talk about it a little later. In effect the anger has been solved before you go to sleep because later when you talk about it, chances are you'll be friends again. Both people have hope.

Another cause of anger is wanting to win at everything, to be first in line, president of the club, captain of the team. This competitive drive can stem from childhood when someone said we would "never amount to anything," so we strive all our lives to prove them wrong. One young man I know, a workaholic who was ruining his marriage in the process, was still trying to prove to his father he was worth something, and his father had been dead for ten years.

A related cause of anger is our striving for perfection. Many people feel they have to be perfect to be accepted. When they don't do a spectacular job, they feel like a failure and get angry. Sometimes we reach for unrealistic goals for which we do not have the ability, time, patience, or resources to reach.

I'm a perfectionist so I know all about this need to be perfect. Earlier in my life, I might get to eighty percent of my goal, and people around me would tell me what a good job I had done, but I felt bad because I had not reached one hundred percent. Then I learned to give God the remaining twenty percent, as long as I did the job that was expected of me and a little extra. I don't think striving for the extra twenty percent is good stewardship of my time. This isn't an excuse to do a poor job; it just released me from unrealistic expectations.

Perfectionists like me also expect perfection from our kids, our mates, our employees, and other drivers on the freeway, and we get angry when they don't perform to our standards. Perfectionists have a hard time accepting criticism. It's also hard for perfectionists to ask forgiveness. When I teach I sometimes give an assignment to "go out and destroy an enemy this week." It means asking forgiveness from someone we have alienated. When we do this, most of the time the other person ceases to be an enemy. Therefore we have "destroyed" the enemy — and oftentimes gained a friend.

Once when I gave this assignment, a woman in class baked three pies because she was having trouble with three different neighborhood families. She took the pies to the neighbors, asking them to forgive her unloving attitude, and healed each relationship with a pie. The neighbors were mostly to blame for the ill feelings, but God honored her obedience.

It's natural to want the other person to come to us and ask forgiveness first, especially when we feel the other person is mostly to blame. But even if we are only ten percent wrong, we should take care of our ten percent and let God care for the rest. Bill Gothard taught me to be careful not to say, "IF I have offended you, please forgive me," or "IF I said something to hurt you, please forgive me." We need to take care of the things we KNOW we did. We don't have to guess. Let God worry about the other person. What usually happens is that he will say, "Of course I'll forgive you — and would you forgive me too?" There is instant healing.

The big test comes when the person agrees that you really were a jerk in that situation. Our natural tendency at that point is to defend ourselves and point out HIS shortcomings. But we need to agree with him as much as possible.

My son Tim was having some problems with a foreman. One day he asked the man's forgiveness for his bad attitude at times. The man responded harshly, "Don't you ever do that again! That's a sign of weakness." But their conflict was resolved and they became friends. Tim handled it God's way and God honored him for it.

After another "destroy an enemy" assignment a young woman named Sandy came up and told me that the only person with whom she didn't get along was a sister — but I didn't mean sisters, did I? I pointed out that sisters are some of the most important enemies we can destroy. "But my sister is in Texas," Sandy said. I told her that is exactly why Mr. Bell invented the telephone, so we could ask forgiveness of sisters in Texas.

When Sandy called, she had a bad connection and her sister's young son answered the phone and couldn't understand what Sandy wanted. Obviously Satan didn't want the call to go through. But God can overrule him, and Sandy's sister finally came to the phone. After Sandy asked for forgiveness her sister responded, "What in the world is going on up there anyway?" When she realized Sandy was serious, the relationship was restored.

Galatians 5:22 lists the characteristics we are to have as Christians:

> But when the Holy Spirit controls our lives he will produce this kind of fruit in us: love, joy, peace, patience, kindness, goodness, faithfulness, gentleness and self-control.

The Greek word translated here as "gentleness" (it can also be translated as "meekness") pictures a stallion under control. On my grandfather's farm I've seen the power of a horse. One day a horse knocked down one of the supporting pillars in the barn, and as a result we had to build a new barn. But gentleness or meekness is this kind of strength brought under control, and it's the key to overcoming anger. That means accepting everything that comes into our lives as being designed or allowed by God, and to rely on His strength to respond to it all in the right way. It's easy to seek our own revenge, but it takes supernatural strength to give a soft answer, to bless our enemy, and to leave revenge to God.

I suggest making an inventory of everything that causes you to become angry and then present the list to God, asking Him to help you handle your anger so people will see you have supernatural strength. Often when you and I do this, people will want to know about our relationship with Jesus Christ. They'll buy into Christianity if they see it work in our lives—and controlling our anger is one of the best proofs that it does.

PART V

PARENTING: THE PEARLS & THE PERILS

17

FATHER
& SON

WHEN BARB AND I GOT MARRIED, there were no books on marriage or parenting. In fact, we had no idea how babies were started. I thought it was Barb walking through a daffodil field or something. Barb got sick shortly after our wedding, and suddenly her tastes changed. She wanted crackers and pickles. We had wanted to start a family right away, but now with Barb sick all the time we decided to wait until she got better. Strange thing — Tim was already on the way.

I took Tim's birth in stride. I believe infants should mostly be left to the care of their mothers who seem to understand them better. Fathers don't relate well to spitting up, messy diapers, and cries in the night. It's plain to see God never designed a man to take that type of stress, so wives should protect their husbands from this until babies are at least six months old. Once they start smiling, cooing, and responding, then fathers can take a role in their development.

We had some wonderful times with the kids. I was a regular customer of the Salvation Army thrift shop, always bringing home wagons and trikes and other toys to fix up. We played golf on the lawn, slid down an old slide into a small swimming pool, went camping, and in general had lots of fun. But as I look back, I think I failed Tim as he was growing up by not allowing him to be little the way my parents had allowed me to be little. Because he was our firstborn, I always considered him more "grown up" than he really was.

Tim has a sensitive spirit just like mine, but I didn't recognize it. We would play Old Maid, and if he got the old maid card, tears would begin gathering in his eyes. Our self-confident daughter Bev would then try to get the card from him to make him feel better.

Tim has been big his whole life. As he was growing up, people would say to him "You're going to be a football player, aren't you?" One day he asked us, "Do I HAVE to be a football player?" We said no, but he did try football and also wrestling. Because Tim has the gift of mercy, as he would get his opponent just about pinned he would let him go. He felt sorry for him. That did not thrill his coach, so Tim retired from wrestling.

We had no idea Tim was a right-brain creative child, and a dreamer. He always seemed a half-step out of phase with the rest of the family. If we wanted to go to the zoo, he would want to go to the beach. If we wanted to look at slides, he would want to watch a movie. If I wanted him to mow the lawn, he decided to clean the garage. He took apart every piece of machinery, clock, toaster, recorder and toy he could find (including some things I wished he had not taken apart). He spent hours underneath his toy car "fixing" it. I only wish I had known what made him tick, and been more understanding.

Being a creative child also caused Tim problems at school. Our schools are based on left-brain subjects like math, spelling, reading, physics, chemistry, grammar, and so on. The right-brain subjects — art, music, crafts, and so on — are things you take if you can't hack it in the usual subjects (or at least that's the way schools were in my generation). The right-brain, creative people — entrepreneurs, artists, dreamers, and so on — have trouble with grades, and yet they're the ones who grow up and change the world for the better.

Tim has turned out to be a wonderful person, though he went through tough years as a teenager. That's typical for those years, though the problems some teenagers face make Tim's struggles pale by comparison.

Beginning in the seventh grade or so, Tim began removing himself from family activities. Although we didn't know it at the time, he was beginning to smoke and wanted to hide it. Not knowing what the Bible said about child-raising, I had violated biblical principles of understanding my family. Like any father, I wanted a better relationship with my child, but I didn't realize I needed to invest time in getting to know how Tim was put together. I had to learn the hard way, through mistakes.

He got into the wrong crowd because they accepted him for who he was. He loved to help people in trouble, and this helped cement their relationships. He was a wonderful kid, but just a little out of step with the family and we didn't know why.

When Tim was in junior high, he began having some hassles with his mom. I took up an offense for Barb, and cut off a meaningful relationship with him. Since then, Bill Gothard has taught me what happened. When someone we love is going through a conflict with another person, God gives our loved one the grace to handle it. But an onlooker often gets all tied up in knots. When the conflict gets solved, the onlooker is still left with the problem. He has not been released. I should have expressed my sadness and displeasure at how Tim was treating his mother, but maintained an open relationship with him. Basing my love on Tim's performance, I failed him — and have asked his forgiveness for my stupidity and ignorance. I had no idea how to discipline, so I just punished.

Unlike Tim, I grew up on a farm in the summers. I had lots of work to do — feed the chickens, cows, horses and pigs, clean out the barn, water the garden, gather the eggs, and pick the apples. There was no time for "I don't feel like it" or "I'll do it tomorrow." I did the chores because that was why I was there; besides, the cows, chickens, horses and pigs were a bunch of tattletales, and would complain loudly if I didn't feed them on time. I thought Tim should work hard too, but we were city slickers now, and there wasn't all that much for city kids to do. There was the garbage, however, so that seemed a good place to begin responsibility training.

Tim was in first grade when I assigned him the garbage. I would casually mention, "Tim, the garbage is getting a little full. Would you please empty it after school?" School came and went. "Tim, would you empty the garbage before dinner, please?" Dinner came and went. "Tim, before you go to bed, would you please take out the garbage." Bedtime came and went. "Tim, before you leave for school (I'm louder now), *would you please take out the garbage?*" School came and went. "TIM, IF YOU DON'T GET THE DUMB GARBAGE EMP-TIED BEFORE DINNER, I'll HAVE YOUR HIDE!" Dinner came and went, and because I didn't know what "having his hide" really meant, and the garbage was smelling a bit by this time, I took out the garbage myself and became more frustrated and bitter as the battle started all over again.

Once when Tim did take out the garbage on his own without being asked, I failed him in my response. I said something like, "Well, it's about time." I should have praised him and bronzed the garbage, invited the neighbors over, built an honorary platform for him in the street, and had the Blue Angels do a fly-over. Thirty years later he would STILL be coming over just to take out our garbage. (As Tim was proofreading this book for me, he assured me he took out the garbage lots of times...when his MOM asked. I guess he and I had a power struggle going.)

Another way I failed Tim was by not allowing him to ex-press his feelings. Because I hate conflict and confrontation with every fiber of my being, when Tim expressed anger I would tell him to be quiet, to go to his room, or to quit talk-ing to his mother like that. I made no effort to find out what was bugging him. I saw symptoms that something was wrong, but could never quite fight my way through feelings of anger to get to the root of the matter.

The power struggle between us came to my attention when it was Tim's turn to do the dinner dishes. By ten o'clock he would still not have them done, though he stayed right there in the kitchen. I don't know how he passed the time, except he did rig up a complicated speaker and head-phone system so he could listen to his tapes or the radio while he was "slaving" away. Our whole evening was consumed with the effort to keep him on the job.

We had to carry through, because when the child constantly wins in a power struggle with his parents, he loses respect for authority. We have a whole generation of young people running around with no respect for authority. They boo the politicians introduced at ball games, shake their fists at the police, and grow pot in their gardens. This attitude begins at home.

I made a wooden paddle with Tim's name on one side and Bev's on the other. Tim thought his side was worn a little more than Bev's, but I don't remember using it on either one of them. Its visibility was enough.

I remember one time we heard Bev crying in the bedroom, and as usual we called out, "Tim, stop hitting your sister." But her crying continued, so we dropped what we were doing and went to the bedroom and found Bev pounding her fists into Tim, yelling at the top of her voice.

We probably punished Tim in error many times. I really don't know how he made it. Yet he looks back on his upbringing with understanding rather than bitterness. I got a note from him recently, reminding me once again that he felt I did what I thought best in raising him. Now that he's a father, I think he has even more understanding.

The problem was one of trust. He would try to talk his way out of something, and we would find out later he had fibbed. Then we would trust him a little less. "You don't trust me," he would say, and I would reply, "You are not trustworthy." To which he replied, "But you don't trust me," with my reply, "But you are not trustworthy" and on and on. It is up to the parent to break that cycle. You have to trust one more time. So you get burned again. Your response? Trust one more time. Sooner or later, success will come.

Peter once asked Jesus,

"Sir, how often should I forgive a brother who sins against me? Seven times?" "No!" Jesus replied, "seventy times seven." (Matthew 18:21-22)

Tim once did something that caused us to remove his driving privileges. I told him he could drive his car again if he would go through the Book of Proverbs, write out every verse with the word "son" in it, and then explain to me what it meant. He took his Bible to school, worked on it after he got home, studied, and wrote, and finally one morning at 6:30 he was ready to give his report.

Right away I noticed he had missed a couple. After I pointed this out he said, "You mean I have to do them even if they don't apply?" Of course, the ones he missed were the very ones he needed, and the ones that applied the most to his situation.

He returned to the Bible and in a few days came back with the project completed. We both sat there with tears as he explained what the Bible said about a rebellious attitude and some other struggles he was having. Later that summer he wrote us a letter, asking us to forgive him for his "tongue," and told us how much the Proverbs study had meant.

The same study works for a daughter too. Just have her substitute the word "daughter" where Proverbs says "son." The principles are still the same. Parents have to get up out of their easy chairs, out from behind their newspapers, and take a trip somewhere — perhaps to the bathroom, bedroom, basement or backyard — to make sure loving correction remains current. It takes time to be a parent.

Barb and I had some conflict over how Tim kept his room. She thought pretty much everything should be picked up. I felt if Tim wanted to live in a messy room, it was all right — everyone needs his space. I was wrong. I just hated the power struggle. If I could do it over again, I would work with him to clean it instead of expecting perfection or just shutting the door.

There were times when Tim would attempt to clean his room with some urging from his mother. After he had worked for a while, he would call us to inspect. We first noticed all the things he hadn't done — the junk under the bed, the closet stuffed to the ceiling.

Again I really blew it. I should have praised him for the right things he had done: "Tim, you simply have the cleanest ceiling I think I have ever seen. There's not one thing on it." Had I done this, he would have cleaned one wall, and later another wall, and even part of the floor eventually. We have to be careful not to always be looking for the negative, but trying to see the positive. When kids receive constant criticism, they give up, become bitter, resentful, and angry, which causes problems for everyone.

As Tim approached age eighteen, we decided to release him to be his own person. If he wanted to change some of his habits and lifestyle, fine. We had done all we could. Giving our opinions one more time would not make any difference. So we told him he was now responsible to God, not to us. We would always be his parents. Our home would always be his home. We would help whenever he wanted us to, but he was free to have any companions he wanted, or to come in anytime day or night. Then he began calling us at 3 A.M. to say, "Don't worry, I'm just over here at Rob's." We weren't worrying, we were asleep. We had given him to God. It wasn't long before Tim was home at midnight, then he was in bed by 10:30, then he was in school.

He barely escaped high school, and viewed his diploma as a pardon. Because he could take the engine out of his car every afternoon, dust it off, and make it run again, we encouraged him to go to diesel mechanic's school. He signed up and began getting straight A's. He had hated math in school, but now he was bringing home fractions and decimal problems. I mentioned that his homework looked a lot like math. He said no, it wasn't math — it was piston ratios and valve clearances. Someone had finally hit his hot button. He is now a successful manager of a diesel shop in Seattle.

If I had it to do over again, I would not mention one bit of concern to Tim about grades. For sure I would never punish him for "bad" grades. I just don't think they mean that much, and they surely are not worth family battles that damage self esteem.

I think Ken Blanchard and Spencer Johnson, authors of *The One Minute Manager*, have the correct idea: They say that when a kid brings home two C's and a D, most parents climb all over him because of the D. Instead they should say, "Two C's! WOW!" and then celebrate with a family party at the local pizza parlor. On the next report card, the D will come up to a C, and one of the C's becomes a B. The praise felt so

> **WHY SCHOOL?**—I'm ancient, but truthfully I've never had one person—even prospective employers—ask me whether I ever took Algebra in school, and what grade I got. No one seems to care that I gook Geology and got a B. I had a D in History at mid-semester, and brought it up to a B by the end of the year, but WHO CARES! People in the work place surely don't, for the most part. All they want to know is whether I can do the job. A few employers look at your application form to see if you put a check in the little box marked "Degree," but they don't really care if your degree was in cooking or Afghanistani law.
> The main purpose of school—including college—is to expose us to a variety of possible life careers. Then we go out in the real world and get practical experience from our first job.

good that the kid wants more. But if his parents are on his back all the time, he sometimes thinks ,"What's the use?" and quits trying.

Parents are funny, getting all uptight about whether their kids are going to make it in life; usually they do.

Now as a grandparent (of Tim's daughter), I've learned not to be so uptight — and I have a lot more patience than I ever did with my own.

18

WORLD'S MOST PERFECT GRANDCHILD

IF YOU'RE A GRANDPARENT, what I have to say next may shock you. Barb and I have the World's Three Most Perfect Grandchildren—Kjersten, Brooke, and Cameron. That means yours is number four at best. I have no idea why God didn't give one of the most perfect grandchildren to someone in Kansas or Romania or England. It's one of those unfathomable things from the mind of God. So just relax and accept the fact that God chose our family to have the World's Most Perfect Puppies, the World's Most Perfect Cat, AND the World's Most Perfect Grandchildren. That's just the way it is.

I'll give you a flavor of how we deal with our grandchildren by describing our life with Kjersten, the oldest. I've been accused of spoiling my grandchildren, but it's not true. I have very definite rules that are non-negotiable. I stand steely cold behind them. In case you need to be more firm with your own grandchildren, we suggest our nonbendable rules:

1. No hang-gliding.

2. No running across the freeway.
3. No playing on airport runways.
4. Only nineteen popsicles in a row.

Other than that, we don't have any rules, but Kjersten knows I will not bend on any of these four, and she abides by that. Of course, you would expect that kind of obedience from an exceptional child, wouldn't you?

Someone has said grandparents are created to sprinkle stardust in children's lives. I love that. Kjersten and I have such a good time when she comes to visit. First we have to go "drive" in the car. It just so happens I have sugarless gum and candy under the front seat which she finds right away. I haven't read one Bible verse that says you can have only one piece of gum at a time, so we eat the whole pack.

I put this "Only one-piece of gum" mumbo-jumbo in the same category as:

Don't eat so much candy — your teeth will rot.
You can't have a BB gun — you'll shoot your eye out.
Don't cross your eyes — they will freeze that way.
Don't try on your father's glasses — you'll go blind.
Wear clean shorts in case you get in an accident.
Chew each bite thirty-seven times.
It will never get well if you pick it.
A little fresh air won't kill you.
I'm only doing this for your own good.

After we eat a whole pack of gum, we play hide-and-go-seek as she hides on the floor of the car in the back seat. I look and look and just can't seem to find her — until she squeals or something.

I have some parking money in my ashtray, so she empties that and puts it in her pocket. She has a sack full at home. Her parents are planning to retire early.

Then we go to the sandbox. We have a set of dishes there, and cook broccoli and have pie and ice cream and let the sand run through some funnels. Then we swing for a while and climb on the ropes. Then we work with her backhand on the tennis court where she hits every forty-seventh ball or so.

Sometimes we'll drive to Greenlake to see the ducks. When she was smaller she would run lickety-split toward the water, and just before her next step took her into the water I would gently grab her from behind. We would giggle and laugh and then she would take off again toward the lake. If she had been MY child, however, I would have had three life-jackets on her, and would have said 346 times that she was not to get close to the water.

We had a peanut party the other day — just me, Kjersten, Muffit our dog, and the cat. The four of us sat on the kitchen floor. I would shell a peanut for Kjersten, then one for Muffit, then one for the cat, then one for me, and then back to Kjersten. We made a mess, but it was easy to clean up.

At the state fair recently the first thing we did was have those awesome greasy hamburgers with onions the fair is famous for. So what if Kjersten put too much ketchup on her fries, or ate the mayonnaise right out of the little plastic bag, or finished the meat but not the bun? Scripture is silent on all this as well, so God must approve.

We went to the aquarium and picked up a starfish with our hands and looked a shark in the eye. We were hungry so we got popcorn; then we were thirsty and went back for a Coke. Then we were hungry again and bought some M & M's. By now the gal at the snack counter was laughing, and said, "You'll do anything she says, won't you?" I said "Of course, wouldn't you?"

When we got home I propped her up in front of the TV where we watched *Casper the Friendly Ghost* for the sixty-seventh time.

Then she needed a drink. Then she wanted some ice cream. Then she was cold and needed a "bankie." Then she wanted some grapes. As I laid down beside that little princess eating grapes, I thought of the Roman princesses in all their splendor. I can't even conceive of a reason why I wouldn't do anything she wanted. Remember, I'm supposed to sprinkle stardust in her life.

So what if we swallow the sugarless gum, or get chocolate on our pants? If God doesn't care, who does?

I'm afraid parents do, so Kjersten's mom Tammie and I have worked out a deal where she is to pull her earlobe if I am letting Kjersten do something against family rules. But Tammie doesn't often pull her earlobe. She is very patient with me.

I was feeding Kjersten at our cabin and she was on a little bar we have between the kitchen and living room. She would lay on her back, then on her stomach, then stand up, then sit down. Wherever her mouth was, that was where I put the food. Of course, if she had been MY child, I would have made her sit up straight and not be so wiggly and clean up her plate, and we both would have had a miserable time. I can't believe all the rules parents have that have no basis in Scripture.

Another thing we do together is ride the little battery motorcycle. She stops to have me put in "gas" so she can keep it running. Then we read a book. Then we go to my office where I keep a battery-operated fish on the wall that wiggles when you clap your hands. Then we get some gumballs out of the machine I have in the office. There is a cup of change handy in case she runs short. Then we go upstairs and "do the dishes." I get some clean plastic dishes out of the cupboard and run some warm water so she can scrub them. She has a hard time remembering not to squirt the windows with the sprayer, but windows don't rust. We can mop that up later.

Then she gets so wet she decides to take a bath in the sink. She likes to make bubbles with the liquid hand soap, and uses more squirts than some of you nay-sayers would think necessary. I just haven't found a Bible verse that says how many squirts to use, so we use lots. Occasionally I take some shots from Barb who wants me to use "moderation." We do. We use up only half the soap instead of all of it. That's moderation if I ever saw any.

I ask Tammie to be sure to bring along four changes of clothes and two or three pairs of shoes. Who wants to be careful not to get dirty? After we get dressed, we read another book. Then we have to swing and climb the ropes and swish down the slide. Then we ride our trike. Then we go in the house and play "tents." This is where we put blankets over some chairs in the front room. Then her parents come to take her home.

Then I go to bed. I get reports later that Kjersten also zonked off fairly quickly after getting in the car. I'm not sure that means anything, but I suppose coming from the same family we would be similar in our bedtime habits.

Do you know why I have so much fun being a grandfather? It's because I get another chance. I was so busy being a parent to my own kids, I forgot how to have fun. I was so concerned about making them into useful citizens, I forgot to listen to them when they hurt, and to do things THEIR way instead of selfishly thinking of my own needs.

I don't want to overdo the grandparent thing, but I do want to share with you a bit of prose by a third-grade girl, a selection that James Dobson included in his book *What Wives Wish Their Husbands Knew About Women*.

THE GRANDMOTHER

A grandmother is a lady who has no children of her own. She likes other people's little girls and boys. A grandfather is a man grandmother. He goes for walks with the boys and they talk about fishing and stuff like that. Grandmothers don't have to do anything except be there. They're old so they shouldn't play hard or run. It is enough if they drive us to the market where the pretend horse is, and have a lot of dimes ready. Or if they take us for walks, they should slow down past things like pretty leaves and caterpillars. They should never say "hurry up." Usually grandmothers are fat, but not too fat to tie your shoes. They wear glasses and funny underwear. They can take their teeth and gums off. Grandmothers don't have to be smart, only answer questions like "Why isn't God married?," and "How come dogs chase cats?" Grandmothers don't talk baby talk like visitors do, because it is so hard to understand. When they read to us they don't skip or mind if it is the same story over again. Everybody should try to have a grandmother, especially if you don't have television, because they are the only grown-ups who have time.

Time is the key to raising kids — and maybe that's why God invented grandparents. They're the only people who have time to sprinkle stardust.

OUR
DISCIPLES

TOO OFTEN PARENTS CAMP on the word "discipline," which to them usually means a spanking. Child-raising author and speaker Betty Chase introduced me to Hebrews 12:5-13 as a picture of how God disciplines us, and how it relates to our parenting job:

> And have you quite forgotten the encouraging words God spoke to you, his child? He said, "My son, don't be angry when the Lord punishes you. Don't be discouraged when he has to show you where you are wrong. For when he punishes you, it proves that he loves you. When he whips you it proves you are really his child. " Let God train you, for he is doing what any loving father does for his children. Whoever heard of a son who was never corrected? If God doesn't punish you when you need it, as other fathers punish their sons, then it means that you aren't really God's son at all — that you don't really belong in his family. Since we respect our fathers here on

earth, though they punish us, should we not all the more cheerfully submit to God's training so that we can begin really to live? Our earthly fathers trained us for a few brief years, doing the best for us that they knew how, but God's correction is always right and for our best good, that we may share his holiness. Being punished isn't enjoyable while it is happening — it hurts! But afterward we can see the result, a quiet growth in grace and character. So take a new grip with your tired hands, stand firm on your shaky legs, and mark out a straight, smooth path for your feet so that those who follow you, though weak and lame, will not fall and hurt themselves, but become strong.

What is God's method of parenting? God disciplines us because He loves us. He does it to prove we are His sons and daughters. He does it for our good, to help us grow in grace and character. His discipline helps us share His holiness and to become more like Him.

So why should we discipline our children? Because we love them. It proves they are members of the family. It is for their own good. It helps them grow in grace and character.

I would substitute the word "discipline" for "punishment" in the above Scripture passage. Bruce Narramore taught me the difference between punishment and discipline. He points out that punishment inflicts a penalty for an offense, while discipline trains for correction and maturity. Punishment looks to past misdeeds. Discipline looks to future correct deeds. Punishment so often reflects a parent's hostility and frustration. Discipline expresses love and concern. A punished child feels fear and guilt; a disciplined child feels security and respect.

Discipline is first instruction. We teach the child the proper way to do things. Then comes training. We spend time working with the child as he practices the rules. Correction follows when he willfully disobeys, but we don't correct until we have instructed and trained. Too often we assume children know the right thing to do, when they really don't or at least don't fully understand the rules.

The goal of disciplining our children is to hand over more and more responsibility to them — to help make them independent. We must help them cut the strings. Many marriages suffer terribly because husbands and wives have never left Mom or Dad and given themselves unconditionally to their mates.

Be consistent in your discipline. A child will use behavior to accomplish his goals. Suppose he wants a popsicle before dinner and you say no. He then begins to cry and stomp around. You have had a hard day, and this is the last thing you need, so you finally say something like "okay, just this once — but never again." You have just taught him that crying is a dandy way to get a popsicle.

The key to consistency is to remove yourself from the power struggle. Let the RULE do the disciplining, not you. Remove yourself from the power struggle.

Let's say you want the family home for dinner on time. Have a family council and announce the time for dinner. "From now on, everyone who would like to eat dinner will be at the table by 6:30." Have them repeat out loud the rule.

For the next couple of nights, little Henry is on time, but later in the week he comes in at 6:45 and sits down ready to eat. Big test! You softly explain that the new rule does not allow anyone to eat if they are not there by 6:30. Henry will explain how his watch stopped, or the sun stopped, or he was threatened by Satan, and it was not his fault. Now you can be his comforter rather than the bad guy. "I'm SOOO sorry you can't eat tonight. I know you must be hungry." But make sure he does not eat. Boys especially will miss only one or two meals at the most, and they will be at the table at 6:30 for the rest of their lives.

The chief problem is mothers. We men can usually handle this sort of thing quite well, but most mothers think their children will get beriberi if they miss a meal. Jesus went for forty days without food, so your kid can miss a few meals without too much harm.

If the child eats the soap in the bathtub, he will probably

feel sick. That will be the last time he eats the soap. If you have a finicky eater, give him a small portion of the food you want him to try, and if he doesn't finish it by the time the rest of the family is through eating, have him leave the table when everyone else does. For sure don't give him dessert. Calmly explain that he eats when the family eats. It is his choice to go to bed hungry. After a while he will consider hunger too high a price not to eat with the family.

A friend told me she was tired of being a short-order cook in the mornings for her family. Her husband wanted french toast, one son wanted bacon and eggs, and her other son wanted pancakes. She spent the entire morning cooking and cleaning up and wondered what she should do about it. I suggested she just announce the menu. "Tomorrow morning we are having pancakes for breakfast. Anyone who wants to eat will have pancakes." She did, and there was no more problem. They ate what she fixed.

Go ahead and make your child try whatever you like, but if he really doesn't like it, don't force him to eat it again. There is a balance between having kids try something, and making them eat it for the rest of their lives just because the parent likes it or thinks it's good for them. We need to be as tolerant in tastes for food as we are in tastes for music, art, furniture, or wallpaper.

Try to serve balanced meals, but don't force a child to eat something he dislikes. I've always hated cooked vegetables. My mother said, "When you get in the Army you'll have to eat your vegetables." I went in the army, but took Barb along as my wife to cook.

The old line about going ahead and eating something you don't like "and pretty soon you'll learn to like it" is a bunch of hog slop. For fifty-five years I've eaten vegetables when I've had meals in other people's homes or had to look good in front of clients, etc — and I STILL hate vegetables. There's no doubt about it: Food tastes are in the genes. Medical science will discover that someday, and you can remember you heard it here first.

Our job is to introduce our children to a variety of things

we think they might enjoy, not force them down our kids' throats just because it's something WE like. A dad came to me and said he wanted his son to join the boys' group at church, but the son preferred joining the Boy Scouts. I felt if the boy was forced to join the church group he would become bitter, so my advice to the dad was to make a deal with his son: After he tried the church group for six weeks, then if he didn't like it he could join the Boy Scouts. You can do the same thing with a musical instrument — have your kids take five or six lessons; then if they hate it, let them stop.

Logical consequences is another method of discipline. The offense dictates the consequence. Grounding a teenager for not cleaning his room is not logical. Grounding would be a more logical disciplinary consequence for coming in late. Paying for a neighbor's broken window is a logical consequence for breaking it. So is requiring a child to help clean up a mess he made, or to play in the backyard the rest of the day after going out in the street with the tricycle, or to wear his pajamas until his wet pants dry.

Believe it or not, kids want rules, even though they may fight them. They want standards to live by. When we don't care enough to correct our children, they get the message that they're not important enough to us to warrant the time it takes to get involved in their world.

On the other hand, we need to have as few rules for our children as possible. Yet those necessary few should be strictly enforced. Make sure the child knows that if he steps over the line, he will get his toe smashed. Almost all children will test the rule and put their toe over the line, but at that point many parents simply draw another line; the child will test that one too, and it goes on and on.

We explained this concept to some friends whose teenage daughter wanted to go to a dance. The parents felt it would be best if she stayed home. She cried for hours, but they didn't give in. Later, they found a note which the girl's younger sister and a friend had passed back and forth in school. The friend had written, "Ask your mom if you can go to the dance." The reply was, "My folks won't let me." The friend wrote back, "Just ask ask ask ask ask!" The girl replied, "My sister cried for three hours and it didn't do a bit of good."

Parents are their own worst enemies when they give in too soon to the power struggle. It is best for everyone if they remain firm, no matter how hot it gets. I tended to overlook problems just because I didn't want the hassle. Then after three or four problems in a row, I erupted in anger that was much more explosive than the offense deserved. Solomon wrote:

> Discipline your son in his early years while there is hope. If you don't you will ruin his life. (Proverbs 19:18)

And also:

> Don't fail to correct your children; discipline won't hurt them! They won't die if you use a stick on them! Punishment will keep them out of hell. (Proverbs 23:13-14)

During the Dr. Spock era, when kids were supposed to do their own thing with little or no parental interference, this Scriptural principle was ignored by non-Christians and even by some Christians as well. Our newspapers today are full of stories of murders and violence, the products of people insisting on their own way — no rules, with the "no limits" philosophy, or "If it feels good, do it."

Spanking is the method of discipline most people resort to first, but in my opinion this should be the last resort. The Bible is clear that using a paddle is sometimes a necessary action. When a child defies authority, a spanking may be the only thing that will get their attention. It is for their good so they don't end up in prison or on Skid Row because they had no one who cared. Spanking a child as a last resort to break a rebellious spirit sounds so cruel, but not when your heart's attitude is one of love and concern for the future well being of the child.

There is a time for spanking — when a younger child

(never spank a teenager) deliberately disobeys and defies your authority.

> Scolding and spanking a child helps him to learn. Left to himself, he brings shame to his mother. (Proverbs 29:15)

> A youngster's heart is filled with rebellion, but punishment will drive it out of him. (Proverbs 22:15)

> If you refuse to discipline your son, it proves you don't love him; for if you love him you will be prompt to punish him. (Proverbs 13:24)

And, of course, the familiar Biblical principle, "Spare the rod and spoil the child."

God created a special spot for spanking. Do not strike your child anywhere else.

If you do have to spank, here are some good rules that Betty Chase gives us:

1. Get alone with the child. Do not publicly embarrass him.
2. Make sure the child understands the rule he broke before you correct him.
3. Ask the child to establish personal responsibility for his actions. "What did you do?"
4. Tell him how much you love him, and that you want him to learn how to do the right thing next time.
5. Spank the child hard enough to break the will, but not the spirit.
6. Comfort the child immediately. The parent who does the spanking must do the comforting.
7. Have the child ask forgiveness or make restitution if appropriate.

Too often spanking (or any form of discipline, for that matter) is done in anger. If you feel yourself getting angry, remove yourself long enough to calm down, and then handle the situation.

In Colossians 3:21 we read,

Fathers do not provoke or irritate or fret your children.
Do not be hard on them or harass them; lest they become
discouraged and sullen and morose and feel inferior and
frustrated. Do not break their spirit.

Think for a minute of some of the ways we are provoked
to anger. Some of the things that make me angry are being ignored, not being trusted, being degraded, being interrupted,
not being listened to, unjust punishment, unrealistic expectations, embarrassment, nagging, false accusations, impatience, inconsistency, unfairness, and harshness. Read back
over this list and put your child on the receiving end. Do you
ever do these things to your child? If these things make US
angry, don't you think they affect our kids the same way? We
need to eliminate these from all of our relationships.

The apostle Paul wrote:

And now a word to you parents. Don't keep on scolding
and nagging your children, making them angry and resentful. Rather, bring them up with the loving discipline
the Lord himself approves, with suggestions and godly
advice. (Ephesians 6:4).

It is all right to discipline. In fact, God requires it. But
then let it go, forgive, and don't nag and scold. We need to
have some fun. Change the subject. Go camping. Do something to show the children you really do care, and discipline
is only for a moment to guide them. They may not understand until years later, but they will thank you for it eventually.

Continued scolding and nagging does result in rebellious
kids because they finally come to the point of saying,
"What's the use? Nothing I do is quite good enough. My parents are always giving me trouble for something." We need
to praise our kids as often as possible.

We also have to keep short accounts, teaching the child guidelines and principles through daily situations rather than a few monthly blow-ups, which can actually drive the child further into rebellion.

I wish I could talk with each father in America face to face, and share with him the Scriptures indicating that love is action, not feelings, and that love is not based on performance. A father's rejection could very well be the greatest reason for kids going wrong and getting into trouble. Show me a kid with a poor self-image and a rebellious spirit, and I'll show you a dad who probably didn't care about them, or know how to be their father.

Once we were waiting in an airport, and this little two-year-old chunk of a girl was hopping up and down, up and down. She was doing her best to keep herself entertained. All at once her mother glared at her and in a rage said, "Would you stop jumping!" The little girl wasn't disturbing anyone; it just bugged her mother that anyone could be happy, I guess. I wanted to shake that mother and ask her what difference it made whether or not her little girl jumped. Two-year-olds jump. That's the way God designed them. Yet we parents do all sorts of stupid things in the name of correction and discipline, when it is usually to solve our own frustrations and anger.

If that child continues to be stomped on, make room for her in one of our institutions. Her self-image won't be worth zilch, and hurting people do crazy things to cope with hurts. Our prisons are full of the fruits of parents who made unreasonable demands, or set no limits, or gave no time or love. And yet often in news media coverage of someone's arrest on a charge of murder, rape, or another violent crime, a sobbing mother will be shown saying, "How could anyone accuse my baby of such a thing?"

Self-image plays such an important role in how we treat our children. My impatience came out most when the kids would cry or fuss in front of other people. I would put my hand over their mouths or rush them out of the room. This action was telling my children that other people were more important to me than they were. That wasn't true, but I surely acted that out. Instead I should have soothed their hurts, forgetting whether we were disturbing people around us. Who cares what others think if my child is hurting?

Discipline was often a tough issue for us, as it is for all parents. But I remember how the light went on when I learned that "discipline" and "disciple" come from the same root word. When we think of disciples, we think of the people who followed Christ while He was on earth. He was gentle with them, kind, a good listener, forgiving. He loved them unconditionally. He modeled how to live. I don't remember Him once yelling at them, even though they made mistakes and must have irritated Him. He knew they were still children spiritually, and was patient with them.

Our children are our disciples. In our relationships with them we should be gentle, kind, good listeners, forgiving, loving them unconditionally, modeling the right way to live. We'll get irritated with them at times, but we still need to show kindness, love, and acceptance. We should be patient, rather than letting irritation get the best of us.

I was not attracted to God because I saw in Him judgment, criticism, punishment, fear, conditional love, harshness, or anger at me. I was attracted to God by His mercy, kindness, gentleness, forgiveness, unconditional love, patience and acceptance.

Shouldn't we give our kids what God gives us?

THE FINE DESIGN

THE KEY TO CHILD-REARING is for parents to be in the Word, learning God's principles of love, self-control, and kindness. When we are in the Word, we become wise. God will speak through us, and our children will be blessed by seeing a model before them of the living Christ and His unconditional love. (Those are easy words to put down on paper, but hard to put into practice.)

The writer of Proverbs said:

Teach a child to choose the right path, and when he is older he will remain upon it. (Proverbs 22:6)

According to how I was first taught this verse, it means that children trained in the things of the Lord will hold to the faith when they are older, even if they stray for a while when they are young. But there is another meaning. We should know how our children are "bent" or designed. It means we need to know our children so well we can sense God's purpose and design in their lives.

Some kids are born artists, some musicians, some mechanics, some philosophers, some organizers, some oriented to service, some performers, some salesmen, some clowns, some serious. When we see God's design for them we can guide our children along the path of their interests and gifts, helping them select the proper schools, classes, and hobbies.

It's tragic to see kids forced into a parent's mold — the football-loving father who forces his artistic son to become a linebacker, or the mother who longed to be a recognized musician and who forces her daughter to labor long hours over a piano when the daughter's interest is painting or gymnastics. When these children fail, the parent becomes bitter and angry.

In his book *Help! I'm A Parent* Bruce Narramore outlines six basic methods of discipline. The first is communication. The key to good communication is not talking, but listening. We need to be active in our listening, not only with our ears, but also with our eyes and heart.

Have you ever been telling your mate about something exciting at work or about a hobby project you're enjoying or about what the kids are learning, and your mate interrupts your story to say something like "Oh, I forgot to put in the laundry" or "I just realized it's time for Monday Night Football"? If so, how did you feel? That's how our kids feel when we don't let them finish airing their opinions and feelings .

If a child sees a new toy on TV and asks Mom or Dad to buy it, parents will typically answer by saying that it costs a lot of money, and will break easily, and isn't as exciting as it looks on TV. What they should say is "Wow, that looks like fun. Why don't you save up your allowance and buy one?" This way they remove themselves from the power struggle, they express no anger, and the child feels he has been heard. (Besides, in three days he will want a different toy from the one he just saw.)

Children have feelings too, and yet we become paranoid if they express them — especially angry feelings. We need to be their mirror, reflecting their anger back to them in our own words: "You are really upset at Mom right now, aren't you?" "You really wanted to go to the park to swim today, didn't you?" "You really wanted Sally to stay and play longer, didn't you?" We need to help them get all their angry feelings out, so they don't have to stuff them and then blow up at inappropriate times. Don't say, "You'll get over it," "You can buy another one," or "That wasn't important anyway." This kills their self esteem because we make it appear their problem is a little thing that doesn't amount to much, when they feel it is a GIANT problem.

We need to allow our kids to express their opinions too. Suppose a boy suggests to his dad that they get a convertible for their next family car. Most dads (including me) would point out that (1) a convertible is dangerous if it should tip over, (2) the wind messes up your hair, (3) you get bugs in your eye, and (4) Seattle is no place for a convertible because it rains once in a while. But what we should say is "Wow, that sounds terrific! I can just feel the wind rustling through our hair — and the sun warming us as we drive along. What a great idea." You have no more intention of getting a convertible than importing sagebrush to Texas, but you can agree it sounds like a wonderful idea without having to commit yourself to action.

A child says "Dad, let's take a shortcut through downtown." Rather than explaining it really isn't a shortcut because of the traffic and stoplights and all the pedestrians,

---

DOUBLE DUTY—It is unfortunate we have to rear children while we're trying to get careers off the ground, but that's the way it is. For those short growing-up years, we have to be full-time parents and full-time workers. Later, when the kids leave the nest, we will have plenty of time to play, and if we've done our job, we'll have nothing but healthy pride in our sons and daughters. I've talked with so many parents who are still struggling with their "kids"—yet their children are in their thirties now, and it's much too late to do anything but weep over their problems.

take a trip downtown. Agree with your children as often as possible. You'll have plenty of years after they leave home to do your own thing.

Kids have the ability to solve problems too. I suggest having family councils as soon as the child is old enough to express himself. Ask their suggestions for outings and vacations, and follow through if at all practical — "Where would you like to go this Saturday?" (THE ZOO, THE ZOO, THE ZOO!) "But we went to the zoo last Saturday." (WE KNOW, BUT WE WANT TO GO AGAIN!). You'll have lots of time to do your own thing after the kids are gone.

Let's rededicate ourselves to being positive with our kids, praising them, honoring them, asking their forgiveness when we hurt them, accepting them, talking TO them — not AT them — listening to them, really listening. We should put ourselves in their shoes, feel what they are feeling, hurt when they hurt, cry when they cry, and laugh when they laugh. Kids are a gift from God...and like all special gifts, they should be handled with the greatest of care.

21

THE BOTTOM LINE

TIME — THAT'S THE BOTTOM LINE of parenting. But so many of us don't have time. We are starting and advancing our careers, building and maintaining homes, and continuing to develop relationships on our jobs and in our church and community. How in the world can we find time to be parents?

The answer: By putting the kids before careers, before church work, before social events, before hobbies, before the laundry, before mowing the grass. As they invest their disposable time, I suggest that young couples with children put only Christ and their marriage as a higher priority than serving their kids. Our career should be no higher than number four.

And for sure don't let a "ministry" foul up the priorities. It's so easy to assume that teaching Sunday school, working on church committees, or having a jail ministry is more important to God than raising kids. I don't see that in Scripture at all. Even pastors are told to put their families before ministry:

For a pastor must be a good man whose life cannot be spoken against. He must have only one wife, and he must be hard working and thoughtful, orderly, and full of good deeds. He must enjoy having guests in his home, and must be a good Bible teacher. He must not be a drinker or quarrelsome, but he must be gentle and kind, and not be one who loves money. He must have a well-behaved family, with children who obey quickly and quietly. (I Timothy 3:2-5)

Why do you think preacher's kids and missionary kids are often rebellious and have such bad reputations? Maybe Dad gave more time to the "sheep" than he gave to the family. The kids began to resent the sheep, and now as adults they are still bitter, angry, and far from God.

I met a woman at a retreat, whose husband was in "full-time ministry" but was not providing for the family. She had a small baby, and was on welfare. He was putting the ministry first. My advice for people like that is to go get a job!

Just put your kids on the priority list in their rightful place, way above careers and money and ministries, and God will bless you, though it may take longer than you would like. If you let the grass grow or let the dishes wait in the sink or let the garbage accumulate, you'll notice the results right away. But if you neglect your kids, you may not notice the results until years later when they are in their teens and beyond. Kids so easily get the message from us that they're not very important to their parents. So they turn to their peer group for acceptance, and may never return emotionally to the family unit.

And don't let the world con you into the "quality versus quantity" trip. Some people say, "I spend QUALITY time with my children, even though I don't provide a lot of quantity time." Baloney! What would happen if we told the boss we planned to give our jobs "quality" time instead of "quantity" time? How long would we keep our job?

Child-raising is a full time job, so I don't think a working mother is a good idea. Often it is only for a higher standard of living or a second car or beach cabin. We are no better than the heathen people who sacrificed their children to their gods. We do the same thing, only now the gods have different names: Convenience, Time, Money, Career, Status, Fame.

Some of our children we murder through abortion — others we murder emotionally, when by wrong priorities we show them how much we wish they weren't there.

Don't sacrifice your prime parenting years. Have children and commit yourself to them. For women that means investing in them full-time, at the temporary expense of a career. After they're gone, you'll still have thirty years or so for a career, plus the priceless joy of being a grandparent.

Men need to do their part too in raising and disciplining their children. Both marriage partners are vital to healthy child raising. Both model special attributes children need.

Sometimes a woman will criticize her husband as being "too hard" on the kids. Maybe he is, but you need to discuss these things together as a couple, outside the hearing of your

---

ALLOWANCES—I recommend beginning an allowance when a child is one year old. Way back in the olden days, we started giving Tim and Bev ten pennies a week, and we taught them to give one penny (a tithe) to the Lord at church. They could do whatever they wanted with the rest. Work out what your budget will allow, but be as generous as you can because one of the purposes is to teach children to handle money, and they have to have something to practice on.

And DON'T make the poor kid save up his allowance for college or clothes. Set up a separate college fund, and give them a clothing allowance if you want, but don't put strings on their regular allowance. If they want to blow it on a kite, let them. When they ask for more money, you can be their comforter as you explain they will have to wait until next week's allowance.

children. If you can't agree, take some classes or obtain counseling, and work out some compromises. But men, don't back off. That's our tendency as men, and we need to do just the opposite.

Don't abandon the ship when the waves get rough. Stick it out, and you'll reap the benefits for eternity.

PART VI

DOLLAR SIGNS

22

HOW TO GET RICH

I WAS RAISED IN A CHURCH that gave me the impression Christians shouldn't have any extra money. The closer to poverty I was, the more spiritual I was. I had heard someone say God would take care of all my needs through His riches in Christ, and I also took that to mean financial needs. Because God was committed to meeting these needs, I assumed I would never miss a payment or a meal. And we never did.

There were some close calls. With thirty days' grace on my insurance policies, I often delayed payment. Occasionally I stalled the light bill a few days, or the telephone bill a week. The minute we got ahead thirty or forty dollars, the washer would quit, or a tire would blow, or Christmas would come, or the kids would be old enough to eat a whole hamburger — not just half. What a shock to my budget! But God really did meet our needs.

I had bought the idea Christians shouldn't have anything left over at the end of the month, because I wasn't spending time in the Word to learn the truth. Besides, I had heard of a Bible verse that said money was the root of all evil. Later I learned that "the LOVE of money" and not money itself, was the problem.

Then one day I ran into some of the most startling verses I had ever read:

> But remember this — if you give little, you will get little. A farmer who plants just a few seeds will get only a small crop, but if he plants much, he will reap much. Everyone must make up his own mind as to how much he should give. Don't force anyone to give more than he really wants to, for cheerful givers are the ones God prizes. God is able to make it up to you by giving you everything you need and more, so that there will not only be enough for your own needs, but plenty left over to give joyfully to others....Yes, God will give you much so that you can give away much, and when we take your gifts to those who need them they will break out into thanksgiving and praise to God for your help. (2 Corinthians 9:6-8, 11)

I couldn't believe what I was reading. God would not only meet our needs, but also give us a SURPLUS so we could give it away joyfully. And the more we gave away, the more He would make sure we had so we could give more away. I was stunned. God didn't have a problem with people having money! It was what we DID with the money that mattered.

Some people reverse this principle and give money to get, rather than getting money to give. I once worked for a woman who was always sending flowers to someone, but would get upset if she didn't receive an immediate call or note of thanks for her kindness.

We give because we see a need and want to plant some seeds in people's lives. If we plant a few seeds (give away a small amount of money), we'll get a small crop. If we plant lots of seeds (give away lots of money) we'll get a large crop. But if our focus is how much we'll get out of the deal, the cycle is broken.

We give because God wants us to. He brings people with needs into our lives; we help meet the need; He turns around and gives us more to give out in His name. It's not for our glory — but for His. We are just managers, not owners.

How would you feel if your banker sent you a note this week saying, "Dear Customer: We have fallen in love with your money and are off to Hawaii. Thank you very much." Is that how God feels when we run off with His money? It isn't ours; He has loaned it to us to help others.

The world says, "Keep your money. Spend it on yourself for pleasure." God says, "Give it away to meet other people's needs." When we give our money away, our non-Christian friends often say to themselves, "There must be something to this Christianity."

We need to be sensitive to the physical needs of others, first to members of God's own family and then to those outside — the neighbors, the guy at work, a girl in the aerobics class, the kid who needs shoes. God expects us to do something about the need.

> Dear brothers, what's the use of saying that you have faith and are Christians if you aren't proving it by helping others? Will that kind of faith save anyone? If you have a friend who is in need of food and clothing, and you say to him, "Well, good-bye and God bless you; stay warm and eat hearty," and then don't give him clothes or food, what good does that do?...Faith that doesn't show itself by good works is no faith at all — it is dead and useless. (James 2:14-17)

I've already mentioned that when Barb and I were first motivated to tithe, we decided to give eleven percent rather than ten percent because we have so much more in Christ than the Jewish people had in the Law. Some people treat tithing as just another obligation, and leave it until near the end of their check writing just to make sure they have enough for the electricity, rent, and other bills. If they don't have enough money that month, they may delay God's portion, knowing He is patient and won't zap them with lightning — but the landlord might!

Barb and I suggest making out God's check FIRST. When we started doing this we were amazed. He helped us make our 89 percent go much further than the 100 percent did. I'm sure the car and refrigerator didn't break down as much as before. If I needed a tool or the toaster bailed out, the store just "happened" to have that particular item on sale.

When I worked as floor director at KING-TV, we did supermarket spots live in those days, and the grocery items that had been used under the hot lights could not be returned to the store, so they were given to those of us who had been working on the set. I had to rent two freezer lockers to hold all the hams, lunchmeat, bread, and other things the Lord was giving us to bring home. We've found that this is the Lord's generous way — He gives an abundance when we honor and obey Him.

We don't worry now about percentages other than as a check to make sure our giving is at the level we want. We just meet the needs God puts in our path, and we expect Him to make sure we have plenty to give away.

That doesn't mean I couldn't lose the business someday or be on welfare, but that's God's problem. I really don't worry about it. Our business plan is to have the Lord bring in more money than we give away. If He brings in less, we give away less. We know He is in absolute control.

Recently the corporate headquarters of one of our largest clients took away about a quarter of our income to invest in some corporate advertising. We had to let a couple of people go, and we were listening carefully to see if God was starting to phase us out of the advertising business. He was bringing in less, so we were giving away less. Maybe He was just checking out our faith, because it wasn't long before we had additional business. If God took us to zero, I would get a job pumping gas and be the best gas pumper God ever had. What a mission field — people coming in for an oil change would get a life change as well.

Do you want money? Then give it away. Do you want poverty? Then try to keep all the money you make. People who worship money never have enough. If they earn $15,000 a year, they long for $20,000. If they make $20,000, they feel they just have to make $30,000. Then they feel they can't make their payments unless they can earn $50,000. Money doesn't satisfy. I'm thankful God gives money to people who can give it away. God uses people like this to support His work on earth. The Apostle Paul wrote:

> But how shall they ask him to save them unless they believe in him? And how can they believe in him if they have never heard about him? And how can they hear about him unless someone tells them? And how will anyone go and tell them unless someone sends him? (Romans 10:14-15)

I know quite a few "senders." God has blessed them with money so they can give it to people who are going out to win people to Christ and to minister in His name. Humanly speaking, there wouldn't be many Christian organizations around if God didn't give some people the means to support them. Paul wrote:

> Do you want to be truly rich? You already are if you are happy and good. After all, we didn't bring any money with us when we came into the world, and we can't carry away a single penny when we die. So we should be well satisfied without money if we have enough food and clothing. But people who long to be rich soon begin to do all kinds of wrong things to get money, things that hurt them and make them evil-minded and finally send them to hell itself. For the love of money is the first step toward all kinds of sin. Some people have even turned away from God because of their love for it and as a result have pierced themselves with many sorrows. (1 Timothy 6:6-10)

After John D. Rockefeller died, his accountant reportedly was asked, "How much money did he leave, anyway?" The answer: "All of it!"

People whose focus is money do all kinds of things to get more, including cheating. But Jesus said:

> What profit is there if you gain the whole world — and lose eternal life? (Matthew 16:26).

Wealth can help others, but it can also keep a person from doing what God wants him to do. This striving after riches can be all-consuming and distract terribly from ministering to others. Paul wrote:

> Those in frequent contact with the exciting things the world offers should make good use of their opportunities without stopping to enjoy them; for the world in its present form will soon be gone. (1 Corinthians 7:31)

I know Christians who are professional athletes, movie stars, politicians, authors, TV personalities, and other public figures. Some have mansions, luxury cars, huge bank accounts, investments, successful businesses, swimming pools, tennis courts, country club memberships, and other things that might not appear as "needs" to the average person. Yet these same people make good use of the opportunities this status, position, fame, and wealth gives them to share Christ with the non-Christians in their world.

The Bible warns these Christians who are so blessed not to stop too long to enjoy these "good" things, but to keep working with the goal in mind of reaching as many hurting people for Christ as they possibly can, and staying in the center of God's will in everything they do. The Christians in professional sports have a particularly effective platform. If they say to kids, "Drugs — that's where it's at," then the kids will try drugs. If they say, "Life with Christ is where it's at," then the kids will be more open to Christ.

Remember, money isn't the problem — it's the LOVE of money when we make it our idol. That's when we get into trouble.

23

MONEY, MOTIVES, & MINISTRY

WHEN I STARTED MY ADVERTISING BUSINESS, one of my first clients left me with an unpaid bill of $10,000. I could have told the broadcast stations that my client had walked away, and we would not be able to pay their bills. But the stations had placed the time on MY reputation — not the client's. As a Christian, I felt I had to repay the bills, even if the money came out of my own pocket. Barb was so understanding.

I wrote to the stations involved and explained the situation. I told them we would pay the bills, but could not do it very fast. We began by sending them $10 checks — which must have seemed strange for an obligation so large — but that was all we could do. We continued paying for several years until we had everyone paid off except a couple of stations in Seattle and Spokane. Then one Christmas these stations forgave the remainder of the debt. We were so grateful! And paying on a bill that wasn't really ours may have done more to establish us as Christians in business than almost anything else we could have done.

A few years later something else happened that set us apart. I had inherited a client with the business when I bought it. He was spending around $300 a month. Over the next couple of years, I showed him how well electronic advertising works, and his budget grew to $100,000 a month. One day the client's ad manager came to the office and announced they were going to a bigger agency in town. I felt stabbed in the back.

Some of the media people who serviced our agency apparently agreed. They expressed bitter feelings toward this client for what he had done. I wrote about forty letters to people who were affected by the change, thanking them for service in the past and asking them not to be bitter, because I wasn't. Since God owned the agency, He could bring clients in and He could allow them to leave. My job was to do the very best possible work for my clients, and if a client wanted to change agencies, that was his privilege. I would accept that as coming from God, believing He had something better in mind.

I received interesting comments in return. Most of the sales reps didn't understand, but they knew I was marching to a different drummer and respected me anyway. Later,

---

A CHECK ON YOUR SPIRITUAL TEMPERATURE—I still struggle with feelings of resentment whenever people stab me in the back, financially or otherwise. I just try to shorten the amount of time between the stimulus and the response God desires. When some jerk rides my back bumper at sixty miles per hour, my first reaction is to want to run him or her into the ditch. Then I ask God how He wants me to respond. He reminds me to "bless" my enemies, so I let the driver go around me. Our spiritual temperature is measured by the length of time it takes to replace our human response with the response God wants us to have. At first it might take a day or two to get over it, then maybe a few hours, and then maybe twenty minutes. I don't think we will ever get it to zero all the time—but that can still be our goal.

when we bought our home and God brought in a better client to help pay for it, these same sales reps scratched their heads in amazement. Several called and said, "That wasn't an accident, was it?" I assured them it wasn't. God simply had a better situation in mind for us and used that episode to test our sincerity in giving the agency to Him.

I have complete confidence God has my best interest in mind, and whatever comes into my life will be filtered through His fingers of love. I wouldn't trade that assurance and peace for all the money, fame, or status this world could give. And I've tasted a little bit in each of these areas, so my feelings are not just sour grapes.

One time I bought some jewelry for Barb from a jeweler who knows we are Christians. He asked if I had a friend in Oregon, and said if I did, he would be glad to send the jewelry to him, and in turn the friend could mail it to me in Seattle; I could save money that way, since there would be no sales tax involved. I appreciated his offer of kindness, but because I want to do things God's way, I said, "No thanks. I believe in supporting the government."

The jeweler is not dishonest; he was just caught up in this world's system, and that includes dodging taxes whenever possible. Christians shouldn't do this, however, because we are told to honor the government and pay our taxes.

I once took a taxi to the airport, and the driver made out two receipt slips for me — one with the correct amount of cash I had given him, and one with twice as much. The idea of course was to pad my expense account and pocket the change. I told the driver I appreciated his offer, but that I would take only the accurate receipt.

Every once in a while a TV or radio station will discover it has been overcharging one of my clients, and they send me a refund check — often made out in my name. No one would be the wiser if I simply deposited the check in my own account and praised the Lord for providing funds in such a wonderful way. The station had done its part, the client didn't know about the mistake, and I was home-free. But I am a Christian and the Bible tells me not to steal. So without a moment's hesitation, I sign over the check and send it on to the client.

Not long ago I received a $290,000 check in error from a client. He was paying twice for some of the media I had purchased for him. I could have retired in Hawaii, but I sent it back. I'm sure the mistake would have been noticed eventually, but by sending it back first, I proved that I can be trusted.

Some people may think I have a choice in this sort of thing, especially when the amount of money involved is small. But if I'm going to be the kind of Christian the Bible tells me to be, then I can't steal, just as I shouldn't lie, or be unfaithful to Barb, or take revenge, or get drunk, or ruin my body with harmful habits, or indulge in lustful thoughts, or be angry all the time, or be disloyal to friends and clients, or cheat on my income tax, or slack off when my boss is not looking. These are principles from the Bible, and it's up to me to practice them. In fact, James 4:17 says it's a sin to know the right thing to do and not do it.

All of us encounter frequent "opportunities" to get ahead financially through a "little" dishonesty. How we respond to them is a good gauge for seeing how well we're avoiding that sin in James 4:17.

24

FINANCIAL FIGHTS & FRIGHTS

I ONCE ATTENDED A MEDIA BASH to honor some of the people who called on our agency. The band is always too loud and the smoke is too thick at these events, but I go because I want to love the people involved. As I walked in the door, the girl making out the name tags asked me, "Do Christians ever go bankrupt?"

I had never met her before, but I guess someone had told her about me. I said, "Sure, Christians can get into financial problems like anyone else who violates God's principles of handling finances."

I've known Christians whose goal was money, money, money — more of it, bigger houses, cars, vacations, boats, and country club memberships. Satan dances a jig when Christians have goals like this. When our goal is money, only Satan is served. When our goal is giving the Good News to people, using money as ministering currency, God is honored and He makes sure we have enough to use for His purposes.

Let me repeat: There is nothing inherently wrong with big cars, nice homes, diamonds, furs, swimming pools and country club memberships if they are used in the right way. If your mission field is the golf club, you had better have a membership. If you are a missionary to the yacht club, you need a yacht. God is not broke. He can make money out of rocks. These things just become ministering currency to allow us to relate to a particular strata of society. The up-and-outers need Christ too. It works great as long as God owns it all and we're just His servants, His stewards, His managers, and not owners.

A word of caution, however. I'm not into the heresy that God wants all of us to be rich. This stand cannot be justified biblically. I believe God has designed some people to have less, by this world's standards, so they can relate to non-Christians who are in the same situation. The Apostle Paul said:

> Not that I was ever in need, for I have learned how to get along happily whether I have much or little. I know how to live on almost nothing or with everything. I have learned the secret of contentment in every situation, whether it be a full stomach or hunger, plenty or want; for I can do everything God asks me to with the help of Christ who gives me the strength and power. (Philippians 4:11-13)

To me this shoots holes in the name-it-and-claim-it philosophy. It sounds to me like GOD decides whether we have much or little, and the key is contentment in whatever circumstances we find ourselves in.

Some people are constantly in financial trouble by giving away too much. They are not paying their bills or feeding their families properly, yet when they encounter someone in need, they give away what they don't have. The family needs to come first. After you meet their basic needs, then you can help others. It is all a matter of priorities and balance, and staying in God's Word so He can give us directions for our day-to-day living.

I've noticed that givers usually marry savers, so we suggest that couples have a family checking account where all the checks are deposited, no matter who earns them. Both the husband and wife should also have separate accounts. Each payday a certain amount is given to each partner to deposit in his or her personal account for golf games, hairdos, or just to spend without feeling guilty.

God gave His people some specific instructions about how to handle their finances:

> He will open to you his wonderful treasury of rain in the heavens, to give you fine crops every season. He will bless everything you do; and you shall lend to many nations, but shall not borrow from them. (Deuteronomy 28:12)

This was written to the Jews of the Old Testament, but I think we can apply the general principle today. God wants to bless us, and I believe this might include financial blessings. It doesn't have to be financial, but it can be. When God can trust us with money, He gives us a treasury out of which we can give to others.

This verse also suggests borrowing is not the best plan of action. I am not against credit, but it is a good idea for a Christian to be debt-free if at all possible, and that includes the mortgage on the house. This enables a Christian to still give away his money during a financial downturn, rather than needing it to pay bills. Solomon wrote:

> Just as the rich rule the poor, so the borrower is servant to the lender. (Proverbs 22:7)

Loaning money is a great way to lose friends. Of the thirty or so people to whom we have loaned money, only five or six have made an attempt to pay it back. I guess they see us with a nice home and successful business and assume we don't need it as much as they do. The problem is, the money we lend them is God's money, not ours.

This puts us in a terrible spot. If we ask the people to repay, it makes us look money-centered. If we don't say anything, they're just taking God's money and running. We have had to write off many of the loans to people who have disappeared after promising they would pay us back with their next paycheck or the IRS return that is "coming Tuesday."

Christ spoke often about money, perhaps more than about any other subject. He said:

> And if you are untrustworthy about worldly wealth, who will trust you with the true riches of heaven? And if you are not faithful with other people's money, why should you be entrusted with money of your own? For neither you nor anyone else can serve two masters. You will hate one and show loyalty to the other, or else the other way around — you will be enthusiastic about one and despise the other. You cannot serve both God and money. (Luke 16:11-13)

Christ does not say we cannot serve God and HAVE money. He says we can't SERVE both God and money. Priority number one must be to serve Christ and be a good steward of the money He has given us.

OH, NO...NOT THAT AGAIN—I'm all for creative ways of making money, but I'm soured for life on one kind of venture—especially because of the way it's been presented to us.

Barb and I are always open to helping people with financial problems and questions, since we feel this is an area in which God has given us insights. Several times people have sounded desperate to get together with us to talk about this area, and even though we were about to go out of our minds with deadlines and pressures, we arranged to meet them—only to find out they wanted us to be involved in a pyramid selling scheme. I really resent being used in this way by such people. Every person they meet becomes a new prospect, and rather than encouraging friendships, it causes others to hide when they see them coming.

I had breakfast recently with a young man who was going through deep water financially and was constantly changing jobs. He seemed to think that because he was now a Christian, God owed him more money as a reward for getting into the Word, attending church, and participating in Christian fellowship. He thought surely God would reward his dedication.

God DOES want to give us good gifts. His desire is to give us beyond what we could ask or dream. But God does not OWE us anything. The Bible asks us to be content with what we have, but this command may be the most elusive. Though we should know by now that the grass is not greener on the other side of the fence, we keep looking at it and longing for it, striving to get over there and taste it.

One reason I struggle with the Greener Grass Syndrome is that I'm a goal-setter. The logical thing for me to do when I accomplish a goal is to set another one. Barb, on the other hand, wants to rest (if you can believe that). It's hard for me to sit down and enjoy what I have. My attention shifts to another goal.

I have an elaborate exercise gym — I bought it to put in the basement, but it wouldn't fit, so I had to put it out in the cold, dark, damp garage. I open myself up to pneumonia traveling all the way from our house to the garage, so I don't work out very often.

Besides, I got the equipment because I wanted to look like a football player, but after using it faithfully for two weeks I couldn't see any difference in my figure. So I went out for ice cream and pizza. Why go to all that abuse if it's not going to do any good?

I also have some workshop tools I have never assembled. My daughter Bev mentioned once that she would like to learn woodworking, so I invested in some machinery. I haven't set it up yet, but I will.

I don't think God is jumping up and down with delight about this tendency of mine to reach for a goal, attain it, and then go for another without stopping to enjoy the first one. It is important I be reminded once in a while that God wants me to be satisfied and not always scrambling for another goal. Goals are vital and biblical, but if we don't appreciate attaining the goal, then we probably don't have the right perspective.

Some of us attain goals to convince ourselves we are worth something. I make Barb tired. In fact, in one of our recent arguments, she blurted out, "I haven't had a moment's rest since the day I met you!"

Of course we all recognize that she's just getting emotional, don't we? Her statement is simply not true. I remember clearly that she had a wonderful day of rest on May 17, 1959. And there was that special day in March of '63 when she was really able to relax. (Isn't that just like a woman, to exaggerate like that?)

In Proverbs 30:7-9 we read this prayer:

O God, I beg two favors from you before I die. First, help me never to tell a lie. Second, give me neither poverty nor riches! Give me just enough to satisfy my needs! For if I grow rich, I may become content without God. And if I am too poor, I may steal, and thus insult God's holy name.

Someone has said that wealth is a by-product of the righteous activity of those who do not seek it. It's a trap for people with money to think they had something to do with attaining it. If it came through their talents, who gave them their abilities? If they inherited their money, God put them in that particular family. If they were in the right place at the right time, God put them in that place. We have no right to be proud of our money. It will soon be gone, anyway. We should go about doing good deeds with our money — sharing, giving, loving, reaching out to those in need. That is how heavenly treasure is accumulated.

The Bible tells us:

Sell what you have and give to those in need. This will fatten your purses in heaven. And the purses of heaven have no rips or holes in them. Your treasures there will never disappear; no thief can steal them; no moth can destroy them. Wherever your treasure is, there your heart and thoughts will also be. (Luke 12:33-34)

We can have a wonderful life on earth, doing good and serving others with our money, and a better life with Christ someday for eternity. Who could want anything more?

It is tragic the way we sometimes fight our circumstances. We say we are God's servants, but when the proper amount of money fails to come in, our car breaks down, we lose our job, or a loved one gets sick or dies, we get all bent out of shape. Sure, these are terrible things to happen to us, but if God has our best in mind, we fail Him terribly when we don't trust Him. We have all sorts of suggestions for God as to how He should handle our situation. When He doesn't act quickly enough, we step in and take things into our own hands, or we worry.

> **BURNOUT IN MINISTRY FUND-RAISING**—We've known couples who work full-time in parachurch organizations, and who spend most of their time fund-raising rather than ministering. They're resentful and feeling burned-out, and their family is suffering. My advice to them: If you're miserable in a ministry because God is not bringing in enough money to meet your needs, GET OUT OF IT! You are not doing yourself a favor, and you surely aren't doing God any good with an attitude like that. God directs beautifully through finances. He can make money out of rocks. He is not broke. He is not on welfare. If He wants your ministry to survive He'll do it without your getting buried in fund-raising efforts. (I assume there may be exceptions to this, but I personally haven't run into any.) If He is not excited about what you are doing, He can also withhold financial blessing so you'll be more sensitive to His way. God has promised to meet our needs, and if He does not do that, something is wrong.

When God is involved in a situation, the answers come on His timetable, not mine. If I try to force the door open, and it opens, it may not necessarily be from God. He might just step aside and let me handle it on my own. We need to be sensitive to His direction to know what He wants us to do. And the only way we can do this is to keep close to His Word.

God has many different ways to pay for the things He wants to accomplish through us. The apostle Paul was a Christian who happened to be a tentmaker, just as I feel I am a Christian who happens to be in advertising. I'm thankful God has given us a successful business that generates profits to give away and to pay for travel, meals, conferences, books, tapes, and counseling expenses related to our ministries. We are free to do exactly what God wants us to do because He is supplying our needs through the business.

Some Christian business people even have money left over. There's nothing wrong with Christians making a fair profit. Matthew 25:14-30 tells how a man loaned money to his servants to invest while he was on a trip. He gave one servant $5,000, one $2,000, and $1,000 to a third. The first two doubled their money, but the third servant buried his. When the owner came home he praised the first two and gave them more, but blasted the third, took his money away, and gave it to the one who had invested and doubled the $5,000.

This story is first a picture of working hard for the Lord, but I also believe it shows making a profit is not wrong. Profits allow a business to expand, pay its employees, and repay the stockholders who have taken a risk by investing in the business.

One of the videotape operators at a TV station I worked for was fast, creative, and used his head while he worked. He was always ready, had great ideas, worked hard, and had a cheerful attitude. Another employee in master control did nothing but read the paper and gripe, was undependable, and had a bad attitude. The union said we had to pay them both the same — a tragedy in my opinion. The guy at the tape machine soon lost his incentive to work hard since he was not getting more pay than the guy who was lazy and grouchy.

There's nothing wrong in paying people for the work they do. There is nothing wrong in being paid in proportion to the talents God has given us. It's not what we have, it's what we do with what we have that counts for eternity. Paul wrote:

> Pay everyone whatever he ought to have: pay your taxes and import duties gladly, obey those over you, and give honor and respect to all those to whom it is due. Pay all your debts except the debt of love for others — never finish paying that! For if you love them, you will be obeying all of God's laws, fulfilling all his requirements. (Romans 13:7-8)

Some other translations read: "Owe no man anything," which seems to say we should never borrow money. *The Living Bible* is more accurate. Paul was saying, "Don't keep on owing." In other words, pay your bills promptly and fully.

The two keys to handling finances God's way are: First, make God the owner of our money, with ourselves as simply managers; second, we should give away some of our surplus to meet other people's needs. There may be no more effective witness than the person who gives his money away. Our culture says, "Keep it!" God says, "Give it away!" He will make sure your barns are full and your bank accounts overflowing, so you can give it away joyfully. Then others will see your deeds are as good as your doctrine.

When we give God one-hundred-percent ownership of our finances, we can stand back and watch Him bless!

PART VII

IN THE
WORLD

25

HOW TO CHOKE PEOPLE

WHEN I WAS IN JUNIOR HIGH, kids passed around notebooks with a student's name on each page. They were called "slam books." In them the students would write down anonymously what they thought of each other. Many of the comments were cutting, snide, and hurtful. The only thing I remember seeing with my name was the comment, "He's a good, good guy." I took that to mean I was a "goody-two-shoes" — at least that's the way I took it. I was sick to my stomach, it hurt so bad.

I didn't go to the dances. I went to movies only when we were in California or some place where no one would see us. Dancing and going to movies weren't sins in themselves — I realize that now, as I read the Bible. But I got tired of people with their lists of do's and don'ts, mainly because my list was not the same as their list, and I resented them trying to cram their own taboos down my throat. The church never explained to me why we didn't do certain things. We just didn't do them, and no one knowingly wants to sin. I loved my folks too much to make any waves with dumb questions, so I just stuffed my feelings and went about my business.

There are, of course, many good reasons why we as Christians should not do some things the world thinks are fine. For instance, millions of people disregard the mounting evidence of how dangerous smoking is to the heart and lungs. They continue smoking because they enjoy it. There's nothing in the Bible that says we shouldn't smoke, but the Bible does tell us that our body is a temple of the Holy Spirit when we become a born-again Christian. That's reason enough for a Christian not to smoke. I can't imagine seeing Jesus going around wheezing, coughing, and blowing smoke all over the place; and since we are His earthly representations, it's really not all that becoming for us to do it either.

Of course, extra weight puts stress on the body too, so it's just as bad for me to be twenty pounds overweight (If you're a smoker, I hope that makes you feel better). I blame it on my age, but I'm afraid it's my lack of self-control.

We're all in this together — just different struggles! So aren't we stupid to point our bony fingers at one another, condemning the weaknesses we see, when we have problems of our own?

Music is another item on the "lists" of some Christians. Some people give the impression that unless one likes Bach, Chopin, and opera, he is not really a Christian. There is slight hope for those who like Mantovani, or better yet, the golden strings of Ralph Carmichael; but even these musicians are suspect in some circles. Other Christians prefer Bill Gaither music, which has a little more beat. Others enjoy Christian music with a rock sound, and others like all kinds of secular music — country, jazz, even rock.

It seems to me that music is a bit like food. Some people like broccoli (I can't imagine why), some like asparagus, some banana cream pie, some olives. Taste in music, in my opinion, has no more significance than taste in vegetables. We wouldn't eat toadstools — they would poison our system. We are also better off if we don't listen to immoral lyrics, as they poison our system, too.

Some churches have fantastic music programs, even orchestras. There are also some people who enjoy singing all five verses of hymn number 576, even though my impression is that the words don't really mean all that much to most people. Some hymns don't seem to have much practical value, at least the way we sing them. Much of the music in our churches seems dead and meaningless. We are quick to criticize our Jewish brothers for their "traditions" that sometimes become more important than the Word itself, but we do the same with music in many of our churches.

Rigidly maintaining our lists of do's and don'ts can be the best way to choke people. We turn off non-Christians to the gospel because we give them the impression we never have any fun, and that we're consumed with being against everything.

Don't be one of those Christians who run around with long faces, hoping for the sweet by-and-by, trying to get through this vale of tears with as few scars as possible from contact with the world. A Christian's life should be vibrant, fun, exciting, fulfilling, peaceful, and joyful — and it really can be!

In *Life-Style Evangelism*, Joe Aldrich talks about developing webs of relationships with our non-Christian friends, so the love of Christ can flow from us in a natural, nonthreatening way, and penetrate their lives.

I like to get out and meet people in the media world. I tell them how an advertising agent thinks, and we can work together on problems. I recently had the privilege of speaking to the sales force of one of the top radio stations in Seattle. They were young, bright, beautiful, yuppie-type people. What energy and vitality! — exactly what an old guy like me needs. After I talked, I opened up the session for questions.

The first question came from God (actually it was from a beautiful gal, but I know He must have set her up): "What are the top four priorities in your life?" Talk about a leading question!

I tried not to look too excited as I told them my top priority is my relationship with God through Jesus Christ. Second is my wife. My kids (and the World's Most Perfect Grandchildren) come third. In fourth place is making a living to provide for all those folks. And in the time left over, I write books, and Barb and I give marriage seminars.

That set the tone for the rest of our morning together. I could now talk at ease about being a Christian in the advertising world and how it affected my life. They were wide-open to my message. I was nonthreatening because I think I proved to them I had no axe to grind, and loved them right where they were.

I got some exciting feedback from the meeting. It was one of those times you look back on with such warm memories. Most of those people will never cross my path again, but they have a copy of my book, which explains the way of salvation.

Our message of Christ might offend sometimes, but the messenger (us) should never offend. I think the picture in Psalms 1 of a Christian being like a tree whose leaves don't wither is an indication to us that we need to be attractive. We need to stay up to date. We need to live out our Christianity in a fresh and appealing way so other people can see the peace, contentment, security, direction, and hope Christ gives us.

26

GOOD NEWS ABOUT THE GOOD NEWS

I WAS INVITED ONCE to have lunch with a man whom I had gone to school with. I had witnessed to him on several occasions. He knew I was "straight" because he came from the same kind of home I did with Christian parents, but he had taken another direction with booze, money, fame, flashy cars, rings, fancy clothes, and so on. He seemed deliriously happy. He asked me what I wanted to drink. I tried to defer to him, but he insisted, so I ordered my usual Coke. He hesitated for a while and then ordered a Coke, too.

The waitress laughed so hard she nearly split her dress. "You? A Coke?" This was his favorite restaurant, and she knew very well what he drank every day.

I broke in. "Just bring him what he usually has." And she did — three martinis.

Except for that momentary crisis, we had a great time at lunch. He got happier and happier. I did too, because I was loving him right where he was. I'm sure he thought I was going to nail him with some Scripture, or talk about how he was "backsliding," or ask whether or not he was in the Word regularly. But the Lord told me to keep my mouth shut about spiritual things. We talked about business, and the old days, and the things that were happening in my life. There was not one "spiritual" word spoken, as I remember.

Just as he left he looked at me and said, "We've got to get together again soon and talk about some personal things." I knew what he meant. The door was open for our next time together. He expected condemnation and rejection. I just gave him love. God will provide additional opportunities to get into spiritual things — on His timetable, when the time is right. My job is to be available, and nearby.

I had breakfast with a young man recently who felt a desire to join a Christian organization, yet had some doubts about leaving his secular job. The more we talked the more obvious it became to both of us that he already had a tremendous mission field. He told me story after story of people who had come to know the Lord through his witness. He also had a great opportunity to advance quickly in the company and influence its direction. I haven't seen him since the day we had breakfast, but when he left that morning he was convinced he could touch many more lives through his secular job than he could with the Christian organization.

I don't consider working in a Christian organization — even on a mission team — to be any more "spiritual" than working in a machine shop, driving a truck, being a nurse, or running an advertising agency. It really doesn't matter where we are. God has a mission field for us, and personally I feel one of the biggest mission fields today is among the hurting, searching, stress-filled people in business.

Our world can't understand the Christian's willingness to tell others about Christ. Religion is a private matter, we are told. But God commands Christians to share the Good News; furthermore, I believe hell and eternal punishment are real, just as heaven is also a reality. God is just and fair, and everything He does is right, regardless of what man thinks or how foolish it sounds.

A Christian who manages a small business told me the other day that some of his employees were complaining about a co-worker who kept bugging them with the Bible. He wanted to know whether he should encourage the Christian to keep on in the manner he was, or ask him to stop. I advised him to ask the Christian to back off. I don't believe in bugging people to receive Christ. I think evangelism must be a natural part of our lives, like eating and breathing, and we need to use God's opportunities rather than manufactured ones.

I had learned isolated verses of Scripture during my growing up years, and I had a feeling I was supposed to sit down next to some guy on the bus, spout off John 3:16 at him, and he would fall on his knees and receive Christ. It never quite happened that way.

TIPSY DRIVER— Barb and I were on a trip to a resort hotel when two of our non-Christian friends—whom we had wanted to get together with for a long time—phoned and asked us out for dinner. As we met them in the hotel parking lot so we could ride with them to the restaurant, we realized our friend was half-drunk (we knew he had an alcohol problem). We were taking his car and he wanted to drive, and since this was his "treat," Barb and I just got in the back seat and away we went.

As we often do when we're with another couple, Barb and I began talking about some of the marriage insights we have gained through hard work and failures. In a few minutes, they were also revealing some things about their relationship, being more honest and open about it than perhaps they had ever been. He weaved a little as he drove (fortunately, hardly anyone else was on the road—I guess God was out ahead of us). But I was sure that God wanted us to honor our friends, and I trusted Him to take care of us.

Over dinner we had a wonderful time talking with them about what the Lord was doing in our lives, and they both listened. We consider such witnessing as seed-planting. Maybe someone else will have the privilege of "harvesting."

On the other hand, no one has ever been led to the Lord through another person's silence. Here, as in every area of our lives, balance is a principle the Bible stresses over and over.

Suppose you are walking down the street and see a beautiful home. You hear people inside having a great time — laughing and talking. You would hesitate to knock on the door without an invitation. But if the roof were on fire, you wouldn't waste a minute getting them the message, would you?

We have so many people coming in and out of our lives daily, and effective witnessing usually begins with being friends with these people.

Non-Christians will never accept God's special plan unless someone tells them about it in a loving, natural, nonthreatening way.

In a time management seminar I attended I was told to begin placing a star each day beside the hardest and most unpleasant task on my "to-do" list. I was to do that task first each morning, and then the rest of my day would be a breeze. It's true. We should witness to the "tough" folks first — our own neighbors — and the rest of the world will be a piece of cake.

Paul used the analogy of planting to describe the gospel message:

> My work was to plant the seed in your hearts, and Apollos' work was to water it, but it was God, not we, who made the garden grow in your hearts. The person who

---

MIRACLES TODAY—God still performs miracles. In fact, some of His most spectacular miracles are happening today—I'm speaking of the lives He changes. The miracles the Holy Spirit performs today can be seen in the lives of people—anger is controlled, marriages are healed, love replaces hate, and people learn to be servants. These are all miracles because they are so contrary to our natural way of doing things.

does the planting or watering isn't very important, but God is important because he is the one who makes things grow. Apollos and I are working as a team, with the same aim, though each of us will be rewarded for his own hard work. We are only God's co-workers. You are God's garden, not ours; you are God's building, not ours. (1 Corinthians 3:6-9)

We can't all be harvesters. Some of us plant seeds — a word here, a word there, a loving deed, a touch of concern. Then some others come along and water the seed to help it sprout. The Holy Spirit helps it begin to grow and mature. We are God's helpers — nothing else — his co-workers. The person with whom we share Christ is God's garden, His building. He is the one who brings in the harvest. As we use our special abilities and gifts in seed-planting and watering, God receives the honor and blessing during the harvest.

27

NOT TALK
BUT POWER

IT'S TERRIBLY EASY for someone to begin reading his own press clippings and say to God, "You are really lucky to have me on Your team."

A true servant is hardly noticed. He is usually in the kitchen or in the basement or out in the yard where no one sees him. The master is complimented by his guest for a delicious dinner, but it was really the servant who prepared it.

Our purpose is to honor Christ, not to bring honor on ourselves. If our attitudes are right before God, He will honor us at the right place and time. We should not seek honor from men — only from God. Pride is nauseating to God. It's so natural for us to want honor for ourselves and we long for people to say our name or introduce us out of a crowd.

It isn't natural to rejoice when someone else gets the credit for something we have done. The religious leaders of Jesus' day brought attention to themselves when they gave to the poor or prayed or fasted. The Bible says that such glory-seekers have received all the reward they will ever get. But when we do things in secret, or behind the scenes, or with the attitude that we don't need to be noticed, then God honors us. And I would much rather be honored by God than by man.

Paul said that "the Kingdom of God is not just talking; it is living by God's power." The more I study the Bible, the more I'm impressed with God's concern for our behavior and good deeds. He tells us to love, to be a servant, to be forgiving — things that are action, not just talk.

If our behavior doesn't change after we receive Christ, something's wrong. We're no different from our non-Christian friends, who are looking to see a change in our lives because of our stated relationship to Christ. If Christianity doesn't change lives, the world doesn't need Christianity.

The reason we are left here on earth is because God has others with whom He wants us to share the wonderful news of Christ. Our purpose for being here is not just to do advertising, or turn out washing machine parts, or sell soup, or be a homemaker, or run a bulldozer. Our greater purpose is to live Christ in the eyes of people so they will want to know more about why we are different.

Christ didn't spend much time behind a pulpit. He was in the street surrounded by the hurting people who could

---

GOOD SEED— Many of the new Christians Barb and I know have had some kind of spiritual background, even if very slight. A praying mother, a Sunday school teacher or church youth worker, a witnessing uncle or neighbor—someone had exposed them to God's principles in early life, and now they are finding Christ, often after a long "exile."

When people like this "return to the fold," what is often the case is that in their youth they followed their parents' faith or lifestyle, but they themselves were not true Christians. After years of neglect and rebellion, their interest in spiritual things is renewed, and this time they truly commit their lives to Christ—and we see their lives change.

relate to his love and care. We have to be real, and that includes admitting our faults, our anger and our struggles, in
the process of allowing God to change those things.

What we do, how we live, our attitude, our priorities, all
reflect on Jesus Christ. Some of the people in our lives
wouldn't be caught dead in a church or listening to the local
Christian radio station, or watching Billy Graham on TV.
Their only exposure to the Good News might be what we
live before them, and the words we share with them. We are
ambassadors for Christ — what an honor! As Paul wrote,

> We try to live in such a way that no one will ever be of-
> fended or kept back from finding the Lord by the way we
> act, so that no one can find fault with us and blame it on
> the Lord. In fact, in everything we do we try to show that
> we are true ministers of God. We patiently endure suffer-
> ing and hardship and trouble of every kind. (2 Corinthi-
> ans 6:3-4)

If our lives are full of bitterness, anger, lust, dishonesty,
laziness, and lying, and the people around us know that we
are Christians, we could easily hinder them from thinking
that receiving Christ would make any difference in their
lives. The more I read the Bible, the more I notice the thread
running through it — good works, deeds of kindness, obedience, good behavior — *DOING!* Our lifestyle shouts to the
housetops who we really are.

When we endure hardship, suffering, and trouble, confident that God has a reason and purpose for our lives, people
can't help but notice the supernatural strength within us.

PART VIII

VIEW FROM THE PEW

IN CHURCH: FROM MISERY TO MINISTRY

GOING TO CHURCH was just something we did on Sunday when I was growing up. I'm thankful for my parents' faithfulness in making me go to church because that set the stage for my continuing on the path at a later age, but as far as relating to my everyday life, it didn't.

Sometimes we would go out to visit some friends on Sunday afternoon, but we were not allowed to play ball, read comics, or do any fun things. We just sat around in our "church clothes" and felt miserable. My Dad and Mom gave me lots of freedom, but when we went out, they wanted us to conform to other people's rules and honor them (a biblical principle I did not learn until many years later), even though some of the people got their law and grace mixed up, I guess.

I can hear some of you saying, "Why force a kid to go to church and be miserable?" Well, going to church as a family and being exposed to spiritual things is essential, in my opinion, to set the foundation of a life, even if the kids don't fully understand or enjoy it. Children come to a crisis time when they reach thirteen or so. They feel they are old enough to decide whether or not they will continue to go to church with the family. Any wavering on our part and the battle is lost. It's one thing to step out of church and go walk in the park when the baby has hiccups. It's another to leave the teenager home to watch TV. As members of the family, children should do what the family does, and that includes going to church, whether they like it or not.

On the other hand, when they reach eighteen or so, release them to make their own decision about church-going. They might just decide not to go anymore, but you have to risk that since they are now adults and are responsible to God for their own path.

Ideally, we should make our church programs so appealing to the kids (as well as to adults) that they can't wait to get to church. The young people's program of the church needs to rate right up there among the highest priorities of the congregation. Too often it is relegated to the basement, in more ways than just physically. I can't even remember if we had a youth minister at any of the churches I attended while growing up, or at the ones I attended during the summers when I worked on my grandparents' farm.

I started driving a wheat truck when I was nine years old and worked on the farm every summer until I was twenty. I didn't go to church very often during the summer. Sunday was the only day off I had, and I didn't have the heart to blow a perfectly good day in church.

When I went away to college, the church meant even less to me. I attended church very little until the semester after Barb and I were married. When we returned to the campus after our honeymoon, I had this strange feeling that church was supposed to be important, so Barb and I would go to the 11 A.M. service, and then leave as quickly as we could to get back to our own little apartment.

After graduation, we left for our two-year hitch in the Army, had our first child, and somehow (probably from the good foundation both sets of parents gave us) felt a church had to be a part of our lives in some way.

After we settled into our Army housing at Fort Bragg, North Carolina, we were driving around the nearby city of Fayetteville one day and saw a sign: "Snyder Memorial Baptist Church." The name "Snyder" somehow attracted us, so we decided one Sunday to try it. The sun was warm that day as we approached this beautiful brick church with a Southern-style white steeple, just like those we had seen in magazines. As we left the morning service, we were surrounded by young couples our own age, many of them Army couples with whom we had much in common. They invited us to get involved socially with their young marrieds' class. I've never been outgoing, but we accepted one of these first invitations to a church social. We got to the church and looked in the window at the group of people having fun — but we had a baby in our arms and felt out of place, so we went home. I'm sure this wasn't Barb's choice, since she had more self-confidence than I did, but she was willing to let me take the lead. Eventually, however, we did become involved with the class and then began teaching a children's evening session.

As we continued coming, I felt something begin to happen at this church. I could almost understand what the minister was saying, and what he said came close to meaning something to my everyday life. I looked forward to Sunday and to being with the people there. Barb and I began to feel a part of that body.

Then tragedy struck! Our young pastor announced he was leaving to take a pulpit in another city. I was devastated. How could he do this to us? But he did, and my spiritual memory goes dim after that until we came home from the Army.

After we returned home, we stayed with both sets of parents for a time while I looked for a job, and also attended church with them. But since we did not have any roots, it was hard to get involved in a fellowship very fast.

After we were more settled in Seattle, my mom mentioned she had played the piano at a certain church in the North End and suggested we try it, which we did. We immediately felt accepted and welcome there, and attended that church for about six years. Then a group of people who didn't like the doctrine the pastor was preaching began to take steps against him, which included legal action. Finally they brought the activities of the church to a halt through the courts. I wasn't into the Bible at that time so I didn't realize how blatantly that action violated scriptural principles:

> How is it that when you have something against another Christian you go to law and ask a heathen court to decide the matter instead of taking it to other Christians to decide which of you is right?...I am trying to make you ashamed. Isn't there anyone in all the church who is wise enough to decide these arguments? But instead, one Christian sues another and accuses his Christian brother in front of unbelievers. To have such lawsuits at all is a real defeat for you as Christians. Why not just accept mistreatment and leave it at that? It would be far more honoring to the Lord to let yourselves be cheated. (1 Corinthians 6:1,5-7)

I joined the group supporting the pastor, and we met to decide what to do. With unity of mind, and following the pastor's lead, as a group we left the church and gave up all the facilities, equipment, furniture — everything. We began meeting in a school, with some people bringing hymnals, others the nursery equipment, others the Sunday school materials, and so on. Everyone pitched in.

Gradually, after dreams and plans and countless hours of work, we had our first service in a brand-new church building in 1964. It was truly a monument to what could be done with a unity of mind and spirit. I was the chairman of the finance committee. We sold bonds and paved parking lots. The Lord blessed the church greatly, both spiritually and financially.

Barb and I taught junior church, I served on several committees and boards, and we were active in our young marrieds' class. Our dynamic preacher pounded the pulpit a little more than I liked, but what he had to say seemed to make

JUNIOR CHURCH— Barb and I taught junior church for eighteen years, and had a wonderful time with the kids. This was not just play time—you can ask any of our graduates. This was serious business. We had our own little pastor, song leader, deacons, deaconesses, trustees, ushers, and other church officers. They ran most of the service without any help from us.

Barb or I would preach a "sermon" which was designed to match their level and interest span. We had to write most of our own material because there just wasn't much in the way of curriculum for the way we wanted to teach it. (The available material consisted mostly of Bible history, and we wanted a little more doctrine and practical application of the Word.)

We didn't want our kids to be bored with church, so we tried very hard to make it exciting. We treated them as equals. They called us Chuck and Barb—none of this Mr. and Mrs. Snyder bit, which separates young and old. I don't mean kids shouldn't show respect for authority, but in a teaching situation, the teacher must be real, vulnerable, transparent, and on the level of the hearers.

After the sermon, we would have an activity time, and play some rousing games like "punch Chuck in the nose." This popular game was played by drawing a picture of Chuck with a big nose on the blackboard. The kids would be blindfolded, and given a piece of chalk. Then they would be twirled around three times and had to find the blackboard blindfolded and hit Chuck's nose with the chalk. (I hope no one steals this exciting game because I have not had the time to get it copyrighted yet.)

I don't remember ever having a discipline problem. A few kids acted up once in a while, but we would calmly explain to them they could not come back if they gave us trouble, and they would have to sit with their parents in big church. That did it! Instant angels. They WANTED to come to Junior Church — they didn't HAVE to. That's the way it should be in "big" church, too. People should want to come, not attend out of guilt or because they are afraid God will zap them if they don't.

sense, even though no one had motivated me to begin study-ing the Bible on my own.

After eighteen years of leading junior church, Barb decid-ed she had paid her dues and wanted to attend the morning service. Now I had to give the lesson alone. Since no one had made the Bible practical in my life, I looked for my material in books and prepared lessons or used some of Barb's materi-al. Most of it had Scripture in it, but it didn't mean all that much to me. The kids learned something, I know, because I watched them grow. But I didn't really take anything home with me from church.

After I attended Bill Gothard's seminar on Basic Youth Conflicts, I was motivated to begin looking in the Bible on my own for things I could apply to my life. The Bible began to be practical, and people began dropping into my life who needed the very things I was learning. I also began reading some of the books Barb had been telling me about, and not long after that became familiar with *The Living Bible*.

In my excitement I suggested to others in the church that we form a small group to meet during the Sunday school hour and explore together some of these new principles I had been learning. People actually signed up for it, and we began our pilgrimage along with others who were also eager to learn how to make the Bible real in their lives. This group grew until one summer we had about seventy people. I couldn't believe the excitement I sensed in that group! We were talking about "revolutionary" principles like being a servant, giving up our rights, managing our finances God's way, and finding God's cures for anger, depression, worry, and stress. We found relevant Scripture for all of it. One man in his seventies, a leader in the church for years, said to me one Sunday, "This is the first time in my life I have ever WANTED to come to Sunday school." Isn't that the way it should be?

I take no credit for all this, since I had already told the Lord I was no teacher, and He agreed. He was just giving me some practice. He was the teacher. All I had to do was keep my nose in the Bible and show up.

Then we began teaching the young marrieds' class. Marriages were healed. People came to know Christ personally. The Bible became more real to all of us. But one Sunday I took a survey in the class to make sure we were on target with what the class wanted. To my dismay, quite a few people wanted more doctrine rather than practical application. I believe this was God pushing us along to another place. He is the author of change in our lives.

About this time we met Jim Zorn of the Seattle Seahawks football team, through a commercial he recorded for me. It took only five minutes for us to discover he was a Christian. He had increasing responsibilities, and we felt he wanted some older friends — much like adopted parents — who had gone through some things. We saw the need, but we were not going to push ourselves on him. If this was something God wanted us to do, He would have to set it up.

Not long after that, a pastor asked us to host a Bible study group in our home for Seattle's professional athletes. We met other Seahawks as well as many of the baseball Mariners and the Sounders soccer team. Little by little the Lord brought athlete "kids" increasingly into our lives as friends.

Barb and I also began serving as chaplains for the University of Washington football team. Actually I like the word "counselors" better than "chaplains," because we love all the kids whether or not they attend the team chapel meetings.

As more and more athletes and coaches came into our lives, we desired to worship where they worshiped. Most of them lived on Seattle's East Side, and many attended one of the churches there, which we decided to start attending also. At the time, few of our friends at the former church understood our leaving, but we felt "called" to this new church just as surely as if we had received a call to Africa or China. We just had to give their suspicions and reactions to the Lord and let Him take care of them. The Bible points out that God is in charge of our reputations, and I needed to rest in that.

Four years later one of the members from the old church told me how excited he was about our new relationships with young couples and athletes. I thanked him, and recalled that many people didn't understand why we left. He answered, "I know — I was one of them; but I understand now." What an encouragement!

29

UNLOCK THE DOORS

As Barb and I sat in the new church, I kept reminding the Lord that we were there to serve in some way if He had something for us to do, but we were not going to push ourselves forward. I was content to sit and be fed, for I was taking three pages of notes every Sunday and enjoying the fellowship.

Then one day our pastor mentioned that teachers were needed for the young marrieds' class, and asked if Barb and I would take the responsibility. I thanked the Lord immediately for this direct answer to prayer.

As we began teaching the class, more and more loving, growing, sharing, and giving people were coming, and I realized we were becoming like a little "church" — not in competition with the larger body, but in a positive way, as a microcosm of what the larger church should be.

I also read a couple of books that reinforced what I had been thinking about our class — *Love, Acceptance and Forgiveness* by Jerry Cook (Regal, 1979) and the book I mentioned earlier by Joe Aldrich, *Life-Style Evangelism* (Multnomah, 1981). I highly recommend both of them.

Dr. Aldrich described many churches as being like a beautiful new department store that carried only the finest quality products, and hired only the most professional employees — but the employees lock the door and sell the products only to one another! When outsiders come to our "store" window and ask, "What's going on around here?" many churches reply, "You have an alcohol problem, don't you? You're also living with your girlfriend, your hair is a bit longer than we like around here, and you smoke — but as soon as you get your life straightened out, you can come in and fellowship with us."

That is exactly the OPPOSITE of what Christ teaches the church to be. He took lots of shots from the "church" folks in His day about being a "friend of sinners." But what a PRIVILEGE it is for us to be friends of sinners and of non-Christians, just as He was. We have a message that will change their lives! They don't know if it works until they have a close-up view of how we deal with life. The church needs to be the place where the oppressed, the depressed, the sad, the downtrodden, the people with AIDS, the prostitutes, the thieves — and the garden-variety sinners as well — can come and find rest, security, hope, peace, and meaning for their lives.

Hebrews 11 lists people of faith that we tend to think of as superstars — we picture them with halos, somehow above being human. I suggest you look closer. What you'll find are regular sinners: murderers, adulterers, prostitutes, liars, thieves, and cheaters. I'm so glad the Bible portrays real people with all their zits and failures. Then I can relate to them in their struggles.

The Bible of course is the most authoritative book on the subject of the church, and among its insights are these from the apostle Paul:

> For I long to visit you so that I can impart to you the faith that will help your church grow strong in the Lord. Then,

too, I need your help, for I want not only to share my
faith with you but to be encouraged by yours: Each of us
will be a blessing to the other. (Romans 1:11-12).

Paul wanted to visit Rome to give the people a spiritual
message of some kind, a gift of faith or insight. As he thinks
about his trip, he is also excited about the encouragement he
is going to receive in return from his fellow Christians there.
It is part of the church's job to encourage one another, support one another, believe in one another, and give unconditional love, so all can be built up and then return to the world
to fight the battles once more.

Paul also wrote:

He will give eternal life to those who patiently do the will
of God, seeking for the unseen glory and honor and eternal life that he offers. (Romans 2:7)

This verse brings to mind an older lady in one of the
churches Barb and I attended several years ago. She stood by
the door after every service, greeting the members and
paying special attention to strangers, making everyone feel
wanted and accepted. We'll never read about her in *Christianity Today* or *Moody Monthly*. We will never see her on TV
with Billy Graham. And, to be honest, I can't even remember
her name — but God does! She was not seeking to be noticed.
Her mission was to do God's will for her life — simply making people feel special.

It is not our visibility that counts, contrary to what I see
in the lives of some Christian leaders. It is our faithfulness to
exercise our gifts, whatever they might be.

It is also possible to force ourselves into ministries requiring spiritual gifts that we don't have. I know an assistant
pastor who thinks he has the gift of teaching. He gives it a
good try, but the classes dwindle in size until only a few
people are left. However he has great ideas and good
organizational ability. Yet instead of going with his obvious
gift of administration, he forces his way into teaching situa-

tions, making it hard for everyone concerned.

Sometimes this "unseen glory and honor" involves out-siders. Barb and I once hosted a wedding. In the middle of the service, three dirty, shabby-looking people slipped into the church and stood for a few minutes, wondering whether to run or hide. I greeted them in a soft voice, learned their names, and found a place for them to sit. During the recep-tion they stood all alone in one corner. I talked with them again, and the bride greeted them, but otherwise not one person in a group of several hundred made any effort to make them feel welcome. It was sad. People need to be over-whelmed with love when they enter a church, no matter how they look, smell, or act.

One of the best ways to get someone's attention is to help meet his needs. Paul wrote:

> When God's children are in need, you be the one to help them out. And get into the habit of inviting guests home for dinner, or if they need lodging, for the night. (Romans 12:13)

There would be no need for a welfare system if the church was doing its part. Someone once asked a group of people how many of them thought the government would meet their needs if they needed help. About ninety percent of the people responded yes. Then they were asked how many thought a church would take care of their needs in a crisis, and only five percent said yes.

What a sad commentary! The church should be first in line. If someone has a flat tire on the freeway, we should be the first to stop and help. If a neighbor needs money to help pay his rent, we should be the first to reach out with some dollars. If we see someone who is lonely, we should be the first to give comfort. If we see someone who is downhearted, we should be the first to encourage.

I can understand why some people are reluctant to tell others about their needs, whether spiritual, financial, emo-tional, or material. I've always had a problem asking for help.

Once I had a flat tire on the freeway not far from where a friend lived. But instead of calling my friend for help, I walked a few miles to a gas station. Later Barb asked me why I didn't call Darrell. I didn't have a good answer. Then she said, "If Darrell was in the same situation you were, would you have wanted him to call you?" Of course I would! I guess it was plain old pride that kept me from asking for help. I love to give help, but hate to ask for help.

Since so many people feel the same way, we need to listen for hidden messages, watch for body language, and ask appropriate questions to determine when people are in need. Then we should follow up on our feelings. God will show what our role should be in that person's life. That doesn't mean we pry into the affairs of everyone we meet. But God will give us a special sensitivity if we are open and looking for people to help.

One time we had five Athletes-in-Action basketball players stay with us overnight. They went through several dozen cookies, stacks of pizza, gallons of pop — but we were blessed as we shared with them God's bountiful gifts to us. Even when we lived in a very small house, we made a practice of having two or three couples over for pie on Sunday nights. We were church-mouse poor, but Barb is a good cook and we had some fabulous fellowship around her wonderful pies. We learned that entertaining in your home doesn't have to be fancy.

And don't limit your invitations to just the "beautiful people" — the ones you especially enjoy being with. Make sure you include the lonely, the depressed, and people who might not fit your personality, but who desperately need someone to love them unconditionally. As I learned from Joe Aldrich, our non-Christian friends don't really care what we know; they want to know that we care. We need to find the balance between what we believe and how we live — between our doctrine and our practice.

The church needs to keep its doors open to everyone. We must allow everyone, no matter how "sinful," to come in and find healing rather than rejection. It doesn't mean we have to

approve of their present lifestyle. We can reject the sin without rejecting the sinner.

I don't want to shock you, but I have a friend who is one
of the leading pornographers in our state. He knows we do
not agree with what he does, and I suppose he thinks we are
a little weird to think there is only one way to God, but we
have a friendship. We went to one of his weddings, gave him
a family Bible, and wished him well. We know we have to be
around him a bit for him to see that Christianity works.

Our relationship started when we bought his house. A
few years after we purchased it, he asked if he could buy it
back, and said he would give us a good profit. I told him we
loved the house, but since he was still carrying the contract at
that time, if Christ returned to earth soon and took us to
heaven, we would default on the payment—and then he

HELPING ATHLETES— We have been able to help
professional and collegiate athletes in a variety of ways
over the years — not as ministers however, just older
friends. We're old enough to be their parents, so I think
this has helped over the years to have the "kids" trust
us. (We have one advantage over the real parents: We
don't know what terrors they were growing up; all we
know is that they breathe regularly, and it is on this
basis that we love them to pieces.)

One of the things we do for our athlete "kids" is to
be home when they want to drop by, something we
love for them to do. (This is exactly what we expected
from our parents. We didn't even give a thought as to
whether they had plans for their life — we just dropped
by and they were supposed to be there.) I think our
greatest contribution to them is just being available. We
love the players right where they are, with no expectations, and little by little they have begun to respond to
our love.

We do not have a "ministry" to athletes. We simply
have some friends who happen to be athletes.

could have his house back. I even told him where we hid the spare key so he wouldn't have to break down the door.

A few months ago he visited us again. This time he brought along his photographer to take pictures inside the house, so he could duplicate some of the rooms. I guess he thought Christ was being a little slow.

My friend may never come to know Christ personally. That's not my responsibility. I take my lead from Christ Himself, who spent lots of time with the prostitutes and tax collectors of His day. He had a message He wanted them to hear, and they couldn't hear it if He never had contact with them.

I like the principle of being insulated from the world's system, not isolated. Too many Christians "Christianize" everything within a few years of coming to know the Lord. Their friends at work may be the only non-Christians they see, and even with them they blow their best opportunities for influence. I've talked with Christians who thought the right thing to do at a company party was to withdraw in a corner and not participate. But if Christ was there, I think He would head straight for the bar, get a Coke or orange juice, and hit the nearest group of people to love them for Himself.

If we show unfriendliness, we get unfriendliness thrown right back in our face. We need to be the true life of the party. Drive the folks home who are dangerous behind the wheel. Help clean up. Barb and I witness often for Christ in these situations. Our non-Christian friends know where we stand. We don't have to wave a cross. God asks us to love them right where they are.

Paul says,

> When I wrote to you before I said not to mix with evil people. But when I said that I wasn't talking about unbelievers who live in sexual sin, or are greedy cheats and thieves and idol worshipers. For you can't live in this world without being with people like that. What I meant was that you are not to keep company with anyone who claims to be a brother Christian but indulges in sexual

sins, or is greedy, or is a swindler, or worships idols, or is a drunkard, or abusive. Don't even eat lunch with such a person. It isn't our job to judge outsiders. But it certainly is our job to judge and deal strongly with those who are members of the church, and who are sinning in these ways. God alone is the Judge of those on the outside. (1 Corinthians 5:9-13)

It isn't the non-Christian I have a hard time accepting, but rather the people in church who have unteachable spirits, the know-it-alls, those who are puffed up with knowledge and not open to learning how to live by God's principles.

Many non-Christians are hurting, lonely, and defeated. Some of them are coming to the church as a last resort. They have tried to find meaning in things that make them feel good for the moment — drugs, sex, alcohol, and even work. But they find out those things really don't satisfy. So it occurs to them to look for God under a steeple. How tragic if the first thing they meet there is criticism of their looks or lifestyle.

We Christians get so paranoid over symptoms. Alcohol, drugs, and casual sex are usually just symptoms of unhappy lives. Dig a little deeper and you will find the causes of their hurts. I've heard a lot of sermons on the evils of alcohol, drugs, and smoking, from people who admittedly couldn't get their hearts started in the morning without three cups of coffee.

I get teary-eyed when I read this prose from George Mc-Cloud:

I simply argue that the cross be raised again at the center of the marketplace as well as on the steeple of the church. I am claiming Jesus was not crucified in a cathedral between two candles, but on a cross between two thieves on a town's garbage heap, at the crossroads of politics so cosmopolitan they had to write his title in Hebrew, Latin and Greek. It's the kind of place where cynics talk smut, and thieves curse, and soldiers gamble because that's where He died, and that is what He died about. And that's where His men and women should be, and what church people ought to be about.

I think the reason some people look to the church only as a last resort is that the Christians they have met at work or in their family or neighborhood are the rejecting, finger-pointing Christians. So when non-Christians come into church, we shouldn't expect instant trust. They will be watching how we live to see if this "God stuff" is real.

A sales manager once called me and explained that he was a "skeptical atheist." He said he had read my first book, and had worked with me long enough to know I wasn't a "dummy," he wanted to have lunch to talk about this "God stuff." I gave him a Bible and some tapes to start his journey.

It's a tragedy so many hurting people have to stumble onto the church. We should be bringing them into the fellowship for emotional and spiritual healing. But let's first bring them into our homes so they can sense our love and learn to trust us. Then we can take them along to a loving Sunday school class, and perhaps later to the morning service on Christmas or Easter. Sooner or later they will end up in the church services and take their part. But first expose your non-Christian friends to your love, then plant some seeds, water them, and God will see to the harvest in His time, making sure they have the strength to grow.

Too often we get our eyes on another person's successful ministry and forget the very people to whom God called US to minister. I wish I could preach the Word with practical insights like Chuck Swindoll, or change lives like Bill Gothard, or thrill people with music like Bill and Gloria Gaither, or have an impact on the world like Billy Graham, or make the Bible understandable like Ken Taylor — but I can't, because God has given me a different work to do. None of these wonderful people will ever live in my neighborhood. They will never work with the people I work with, or meet my friends. So there is no way they could do what God has asked me to do, any more than I could do what they do.

When we are all doing our part, we fit together well and are sensitive to the needs of each of the other parts. Paul wrote:

> So, my dear brothers, since future victory is sure, be strong and steady, always abounding in the Lord's work, for you know that nothing you do for the Lord is ever wasted as it would be if there were no resurrection. (1 Corinthians 15:58)

This verse is such a comfort to me when I get tired and want to quit. Since the victory is already won through Christ, I can be strong and steady, knowing the outcome of the conflict. I believe all our efforts need to be directed in one way or another toward loving people to Christ, and this takes time and work. Yet some people waste their time arguing among themselves, discussing things that really don't matter in the big picture. We need to concentrate on building a message within ourselves and within the church and then living that message. The Holy Spirit lives within us, and that makes us His building, His church — and because of that we can change the world.

In summary, the role of the church is to feed the sheep. The sheep then go out to evangelize the world.

Lately I've mulled this over a lot, and I can't think of one reason why a person should stay in a local church if they are not being fed spiritually. I've met some people who say that even in that situation we should stay to support the pastor, or to support the other people going there, or to continue teaching a Sunday school class or serving on a board, or because our family or all our friends attend there, or because we've already given a lot of money to the building fund. But not one of those is a good enough reason to stay in a local church and spiritually starve. You don't do anyone any good if you aren't growing in the Lord, and you can't grow unless you are getting spiritual food.

MY DREAM CHURCH

MY DREAM CHURCH would have a minimum of rules. In some churches the doors are shut once the worship service begins. People who are late are "punished" by being made to wait outside until an "appropriate" time. My church won't have any doors. People can come and go. The only rule we will have is being real in front of the people who come into our life.

In my dream church you'll be able to sit where you want. Even if the gathering is small, no one will ask you to get up and move closer to the front.

On one occasion Barb and I were speaking to denominational leaders on the subject of how to teach an adult Sunday school class. We explained that we always had coffee and donuts ready when people came, and encouraged conversation with one another. This bothered the systems-and-program people a bit because they didn't think we were starting "on time." Sure we were. We were starting on time with fellowship.

I also explained that we welcomed all ages in our class, from grandmas to children. The youth director of our church once said to me indignantly, "Do you realize you have high school kids in your class?" I said "Yes, isn't that great!" I don't think that was the answer he wanted to hear.

I don't believe in age-grading classes. No modeling takes place. If they aren't together once in a while, young people can't see good marriages in action. Grandmas can't teach young mothers how to care for babies. Young people starting out in business can't learn the ropes from more established business people.

In my dream church we won't be taking an attendance record. We won't have any membership rolls either. And we won't be taking an offering. If God wants to meet our needs He'll motivate the folks to give.

We won't be giving any announcements from the pulpit (I assume most people can read, so the printed bulletin should take care of this).

My dream church would focus on teaching the members how to bring people into a personal relationship with Christ.

The church is to feed the "sheep" so they can go out to the advertising agencies, plumbing shops, board rooms, and radio stations of the world and live Christ in front of their non-Christian friends.

In my dream church, pastors will preach from their lives as they live the Word week to week.

I can't count the number of times I've sat in a church pew listening to a preacher talking in terms that would make a seminary graduate scratch his head. Paul said it so plainly. The message of Christ is simple, and powerful, and beautiful. Yet some people continue to contaminate it with arrogant puffiness.

Paul wrote:

For Christ didn't send me to baptize, but to preach the Gospel; and even my preaching sounds poor, for I do not fill my sermons with profound words and high sounding ideas, for fear of diluting the mighty power there is in the simple message of the cross of Christ. (1 Corinthians 1:17)

The apostle Paul told of his desire to keep his sermons on the level of the listener. I have heard more pontifical know-it-all preachers than I care to remember. Their approach only brings bitter memories to my mind of "dying" in the pew, trying to keep my mind occupied, not having the slightest idea what the speaker was trying to say, counting the bricks in the choir loft.

Chuck Swindoll says that when some people can't understand what he is teaching they think he is deep; and when they CAN understand him, they think he is shallow. Barb and I have been accused at times of being shallow in our teaching. I guess it's because people can understand what we are saying, and can begin changing their lives through being

---

LEARNED IN THE FIRE— I've heard the quote, "God doesn't use someone until He has allowed him to hurt deeply." Years ago I would have been bothered by such a saying. Who wants to hurt? Is God just some giant cosmic monster waiting to zap us with trouble? Who needs that? But what this saying means is that you really don't have a message until you've been through the fire. The only time it becomes real is when the teacher can say from first-hand experience, "That really hurt, and here's what I learned from it."

I hate it when teachers get their lessons out of books rather than out of their lives. Anyone can read a book and give a sermon. It scares me to see row after row of sermons for sale in Christian bookstores, because that means someone is buying them and using them from the pulpit without first living the principles to see if they work.

For someone who is doing that, I suggest that he tape-record his sermon and bring the tape and a tape player to the service. The sheep could also bring their tape recorders, and when the pastor puts his on "play," the sheep could put theirs on "record," and then everyone could immediately go out for coffee.

In my opinion, a sermon not filtered through a life is worthless. I heartily agree with the saying, "I'd rather SEE a sermon than hear one."

exposed to God's Word in a practical way.

My dream church would be one in which people of different doctrinal persuasions could worship comfortably together — a place where people could freely grow and learn and love one another unconditionally. The doors would be open to anyone regardless of how far they had come on their path to finding God.

We can worship together even if we don't agree on all the finer points of doctrine. It's pointless to argue. Some Christian groups believe you can never lose your salvation once you accept Christ into your life. Others think you can lose your salvation by sinning. Some believe in present-day miracle gifts like tongues, healing, and prophecy; others believe they are not in use today, and were given only in the first century to authenticate men of God. Some forbid the wearing of jewelry. Some meet on Saturday instead of Sunday. Some require water baptism, and others think baptism is optional. I could go on and on with non-issues that we allow to become major battle grounds while people all around us are going to hell.

Nothing is more boring than majoring on the minors in church, and it's a sin to bore people in the name of Christ.

Let's set our feet once and for all on the truly major doctrinal issues of Christianity — such as the deity of Christ, the Trinity, and salvation by grace. Then we need to go out and put into practice what we learn. We are not to keep going over the same ground:

> You have been Christians a long time now, and you
> ought to be teaching others, but instead you have
> dropped back to the place where you need someone to
> teach you all over again the very first principles in God's
> Word. You are like babies who can drink only milk, not
> old enough for solid food. And when a person is still
> living on milk it shows he isn't very far along in the
> Christian life, and doesn't know much about the differ-
> ence between right and wrong. He is still a baby Chris-

tian! You will never be able to eat solid spiritual food and understand the deeper things of God's Word until you become better Christians and learn right from wrong by PRACTICING [my emphasis] doing right. Let us stop going over the same old ground again and again, always teaching those first lessons about Christ. Let us go on instead to other things and become mature in our understanding, as strong Christians ought to be. Surely we don't need to speak further about the foolishness of trying to be saved by being good, or about the necessity of faith in God; you don't need further instruction about baptism and spiritual gifts and the resurrection of the dead and eternal judgment. (Hebrews 5:12 — 6:2)

I can't figure out how churches can read this portion of Scripture and continue to major on doctrinal issues sermon after sermon. I've emphasized the key word in the passage — we need to PRACTICE doing right. It's our *doing* that makes Christianity valuable to other people. We need to practice holding our anger, filling out our tax forms honestly, taking time for our families, being a good employee, and handling our finances God's way. The key is DOING things God's way, even when no one else is looking.

Doctrine is important, but we must go out and live it. The greatest danger to the evangelical church is not communism or cults; it is the wide gap between what we say and how we live.

Someone has said that most pastors and teachers answer the questions no one is asking, and duck the questions almost EVERYONE is asking. It's also been said that theological arguments generate more heat than light.

It is good to remember that the church of the Bible is not a building. If we have Christ in our lives, WE are the church. The temple of the Holy Spirit is *us* — not the building where we meet. I'm tired of hearing complaints when part of the church building is used as a gymnasium, of all things! "Why, people could get sweaty! And who can worship in a place where people have sweated?" The building is not sacred. It is the fellowship of believers that is sacred and pleasing to God. We might get a lot more done for Christ by tearing out a few pews, putting up a hoop, and inviting the kids from the neighborhood over for basketball, rather than catering to some of the stifling saints.

Change is threatening. It is so much safer to spend our time at church wondering about harmless doctrinal points or about how the building looks, rather than loving an enemy or asking forgiveness.

As we've said, the message of Christ is simple; and viewed from the outside, I suppose it could look foolish. It's hard to explain unless the Holy Spirit is working in your heart.

One writer put it this way:

We feel supreme love for One we've never seen.
We listen closely to One who never actually speaks.
We entrust our destiny into the hand of One we have
    never met.
We empty ourselves in order to be full.
We admit we're wrong so we can be declared right.
We go down in order to get up.
We're strongest when we're weakest.
We're richest when we're poorest.
Our best strategy in battle is on our knees.
Our escape from pressure is standing still.
We die so we can live.
We forsake so we can have.
We surrender so we can conquer.
We see the invisible.
We hear the inaudible.
We believe the incredible.
We understand the inscrutable.
In fact, we know that which passes knowledge.

It isn't hard to see how some people find our message incredible. We need to keep giving it, however, because in His own time and His own way God will make Himself clear to our non-Christian friends. All we must do is be faithful to give a reason for the hope we have in us through Christ.

SPIRITUAL GIFTS & CHURCH RESPONSIBILITIES— I've served on church boards, as well as boards outside the church, but often I would feel out of place. Frequently I thought we should go ahead with a project in which the Lord seemed to be leading, even if we didn't know exactly how we were going to pay for it. I figured the leaders of the children of Israel probably had to put their feet into the water before the Red Sea opened, so I felt we needed to step out in faith on some of the "impossible" projects we faced, and see if God would open the door. After all, we haven't appropriated one OUNCE of God's power until we try the impossible. If we know how we're going to work it out, we don't need God.

Later I found out the real reason why I was so uncomfortable in board meetings. I don't have the gift of boards — the gift called "administration" in the Bible. No wonder I was so frustrated! I was trying to do something for which I wasn't gifted. It's a mistake to ask a person to serve on a board of trustees or deacons if the person doesn't have the gift of administration. Certainly, it would help to have an occasional man of faith on the board too, but we need to work in our major gifts.

I don't think it is wise to put a person in charge of the hospital ministry who doesn't have the gift of mercy. The head of the missions committee should have the gifts of mercy and giving. The effective Sunday school teacher needs to have the gift of teaching or exhortation. A church's spiritual leader should have the gift of wisdom, among others. The finance chairman should probably have the gifts of faith and of giving. The kitchen committee head should have the gift of helps. The chairman of the outreach committee should have the gift of evangelism.

This sounds so simple, and it makes everything run so much more smoothly, but many churches are not matching gifts with jobs.

31

NO
STRANGER

WE INHERITED A CAT when we bought our present home. We called her Stranger. She was skittish and we could hardly pet her, but over the years she finally would come to the porch to get fed. Then a black and white cat came out of the woods, knocked on our door, informed us we were hers, and went over to the furnace vent to get warm. She's sampled fourteen brands of cat food, and Barb even put a litter box in the basement, which was a miracle right next to God opening the Red Sea for the Jewish folks.

Stranger had the same opportunity as the black and white cat. She could have come in and warmed herself and gotten spoiled, but she chose to stay out in the cold. That's what many non-Christians do. By a simple act of asking Jesus Christ to come into their lives, they would have a future beyond their wildest dreams in this world, and in the world to come. But they choose to stay outside, and will miss a beautiful heavenly experience.

The Bible says clearly we can't earn our salvation:

Then what can we boast about doing, to earn our salvation? Nothing at all. Why? Because our acquittal is not based on our good deeds; it is based on what Christ has done and our faith in him. So it is that we are saved by faith in Christ and not by the good things we do. (Romans 3:27-28)

The reason salvation by "works" is taught by so many different religions is that people FEEL better if they do something to earn God's favor. If we suffer, or offer a special service, or exercise some spiritual gift, it makes us feel more worthy of God's love. We like to earn our own way. Most of us are uncomfortable when we are given things free. If we went out on the street and offered people guaranteed eternal life for $10,000, they would dig ditches, work three jobs, and take in laundry and day-care kids to qualify. But when we say eternal life is a free gift, then it is suspect.

"FOOLISHNESS"— It will be a terrible shock for a lot of people on Judgment Day to be standing on the other side of the gulf separating Christians and non-Christians. They'll realize they have chosen the wrong path, the path that leads to destruction rather than to eternal life through Christ. Some may never know they have made the wrong choice until they stand before God and He says to His angels, "I never knew him. Take him away."

I know this may sound like foolishness to you, and whether you agree with me or not makes no difference as far as my respect for you as a person. You have to make your own choice. But God has made Himself so plain to me, and I would be the fool of all fools to neglect such a marvelous plan.

It's a narrow way — no question about that — while the path to destruction is wide. But I can tell you sincerely that God has proved Himself real, so I don't have to worry about Christianity being some cosmic joke. It is life itself and I look forward with excitement to the day when I will see Christ face to face.

No, we cannot earn our salvation by the things we do. The Book of Isaiah says our works are like filthy rags to God. The Book of Romans is filled with references pointing out that it is Who we know, not what we do, that brings us salvation. On the other hand, the Book of James says there are some things we can do in gratitude for that free gift. We are not doing good works to EARN our salvation, but BECAUSE of our salvation — and there is a world of difference. Since we have eternal life through Jesus Christ, people should see the evidence in our lives. We should show a supernatural ability to handle anger, temptations, trials, our tongue, and our thoughts.

If people don't ever see changes in our lives, they have reason to doubt whether we really know Christ personally. If Christ comes into a life, there WILL be changes. You won't be able to miss them. The speed and depth of change and growth varies between people, but there will be evident changes. You can't help but change if you are sincerely seeking God.

That doesn't mean our life changes automatically. It takes work on our part; but again, it isn't the work that saves us, but rather our acceptance of God's free gift of salvation.

32

WHY PRAY?

I ONCE HEARD A DEACON in our church suggest that it really didn't do much good to pray, because God has designed everything to come out a certain way anyway. As I look back on it, he was the kind of teacher who set up straw dummies all the time so you really never quite knew where he stood. It could be I missed the dummy knockdown session, because for years I was inconsistent and powerless in prayer.

I lived in fear that someone would call on me to pray in church. I did not have the skills needed for public prayer, and I didn't know any lofty phrases. I was pretty much a ham-and-eggs-type pray-er, and I assumed my prayers didn't actually bless anyone or get much higher than the ceiling. It wasn't that I didn't have a relationship with the Lord; public praying just felt so fakey.

Once in a while I would attend a Wednesday night prayer meeting. The men and women would break into separate groups. I hated to be away from Barb at church because I needed her spiritual support. I was too vulnerable out there on my own, fearing someone might ask me a question I couldn't answer, or want me to quote a verse from the Bible I didn't know.

As I sat in a circle, praying with the other men, I often wondered how in the world I got there. I guess it was guilt that brought me; this was just something we were supposed to do.

We would all have to pray in turn, and for some reason I was usually one of the last. As my time came nearer, everything worthwhile had been prayed for, so I would sit there and strain and think and sweat, trying to come up with something no one else had thought of, and I would remember the radio ministry, the tract rack, the work party, or maybe the library. Just then the guy sitting next to me would say something like, "And in closing, Lord, we ask Your blessing on the radio ministry, the tract rack, Saturday's work party, and the library. Amen." Panicsville!

In the past I had heard some of the men give God reminders of what had already been prayed for, so I would resort to something like "Dear Lord, as Dave prayed, we hope You'll bless the radio ministry, tract rack, the work party, and the library. And bless everything else everyone has prayed for here tonight, and I hope we don't get cancer. Amen." Needless to say, my Wednesday night prayer meeting attendance was not outstanding.

During the Sunday evening service, the pastor would call on various people in the congregation to open or close in prayer. I found if I scrunched down in my seat and placed the head of the person sitting in front of me between the pastor and my eyes, most of the time I would escape the assignment.

Another thing that bothered me — and still does — is the habit some prayer leaders have of asking someone to pray for something he's never experienced, or for someone he's never met, or for a situation on which he has no firsthand knowledge.

Let's say George would like us to pray for his great-aunt's neighbor's boss who has cancer, and with a tender heart and obvious concern he informs the group of the situation. Then, instead of asking George to pray, the group leader would say, "Chuck, would you pray for George's great-aunt's neighbor's boss please?" Of course I could fake it, so I got by; but how much better it is to ask the person with the heart's concern to pray for a situation.

Some churches follow the practice of reciting in Sunday morning prayer all the various requests included in the weekly bulletin. It sounds like a laundry list, and has about as much meaning for me as the clerk in the Senate reading a bill to the floor. Usually the person praying has no firsthand knowledge about the various people and problems listed in the bulletin, so to remember everything I suppose he has to peek at the list while praying. I even heard a guy pray one time at a church we attended, "O Lord, you know what Plato said when he wrote...." I assume the Lord has read all the great works of man and remembers what Plato wrote. But what does that have to do with making prayer real? For me, prayer means nothing unless I know the subject firsthand and have a heart's concern for the situation.

It has only been during the last year or so that I have been faithful in regular, consistent prayer on my own. I keep a prayer book where I write down my requests, thanksgiving, and answers. I finally came to the conclusion that since I was God's servant, it was stupid for me to go about my day without checking with the Master about what he wanted me to do that day. I want to serve Him in every way possible, in the way He wants me to serve. I'm not sure if it's my imagination or not, but I'll swear that my days go more smoothly. I get more green lights, more parking spaces, more open bridges than I ever did before I began the program of asking God to direct my path each day.

When I begin to pray, it's easy for my mind to wander to some concern at work, or a person, or a situation. And I feel guilty for getting off the track and force my mind back to the business at hand. Now during prayer I keep a piece of paper handy (that was Keith Miller's suggestion) to jot down those thoughts that come into mind that aren't related to what is being prayed about. I don't worry about forgetting them and can go back to prayer with a new confidence. Sometimes God speaks to us through these "wandering thoughts," especially when we are quiet before Him.

I look forward to my time in prayer, but it has taken many years for me to come to this point. I still have some situations for which I'm not sure if I should bother God or not — for instance, praying for sports victories. God has "family" members on both sides of the line, and my guess is that He has to put His hand over His eyes during each game. I'm still not sure whether I can pray for the Seahawks, Mariners, Huskies, and Sonics to win, but I go through the motions anyway.

I guess I've heard more legalistic sermons on prayer than I care to remember, all ending up in a big guilt trip for me. One of my favorite passages in the Bible talks about prayer:

> Don't worry about anything; instead, pray about everything; tell God your needs and don't forget to thank him for his answers. If you do this you will experience God's peace, which is far more wonderful than the human mind can understand. His peace will keep your thoughts and your hearts quiet and at rest as you trust in Christ Jesus. (Philippians 4:6-7)

To those around us who are going through struggles and problems, we often quote the first part of this passage and say, "Don't worry about losing your job; don't worry about your cancer surgery; don't worry about your daughter who is three hours overdue coming home." All we tell people is "Don't worry," but they do worry, and then feel guilty about it. We supersaints tend to waggle our bony fingers at our friends in legalistic piety, and we say, in effect, "Obviously you're not too spiritual, since you are worrying." But people do worry, and just telling them not to worry won't help. We need to point them to prayer, the solution to worry. Our bodies are simply not designed to handle worry. We need to let God take our problems and handle them for us.

Prayer is not a complicated religious experience, but simply the natural outflow of a father-child relationship. When we were children we would often cry out to our earthly fathers, asking them to help in some way. The religious leaders of Jesus' day believed strongly in prayer, but they bound it with man-made rules and traditions that were not based on Scripture. Prayer became formalized, institutionalized, and not spontaneous. A Pharisee addressed God this way: "O Eternal, Matchless, Omnipotent, Ruler, King, Magnificent, Marvelous, Immortal,…" etc. I guess the principle was that if they flattered God enough He would give in and do what they wanted.

I can't imagine my son wanting to talk with me and starting out: "O marvelous advertising person with a great first serve, photographer, guitar player, father, etc., etc. — hear me as I ask you…" That's ridiculous! What he would say is, "Dad, I've got a problem, and here's the situation…" And he would have my ear.

There is a balance. To stand before the Almighty Creator should fill us with awe. To enjoy being in God's presence because we love Him should never cause us to become flippant and disrespectful. But God is also our heavenly Father, and He desires a close relationship with us. Jesus said:

Don't recite the same prayer over and over as the heathen do, who think prayers are answered only by repeating them again and again. Remember, your Father knows exactly what you need even before you ask him! (Matthew 6:7-8).

Prayers in Jesus' day had become repetitious. People repeated the same words again and again. Where in the Bible does it say to do that? It doesn't, yet this is the practice of some churches even today, and I don't see how they justify it.

There is often some pride connected with public prayer. When a pastor or other Christian leader walks to a platform before a giant crowd and sits down with his head in his hand to pray, some may think that if he has waited until then to pray, it's too late. Why didn't he pray in the prayer room where God can hear his requests in secret? Then he can come out onto the platform ready to be a good representative of Jesus Christ — smiling, happy, and confident that God will speak through him.

Does that mean I'm against public prayer? Not at all. I pray before and after every class I teach, asking God to open hearts to what He would have us learn from His Word that day. I pray in restaurants when I'm with other Christians — quietly, no big deal — because I am grateful for the fellowship and the meal He has provided.

If I have any doubts whether praying in a restaurant or another public place would make the people I'm with uncomfortable, I pray with my eyes open, and don't try to force them into an awkward situation. I want to win these non-Christian friends, not drive them away. You may not agree, but it's my observation that quite a bit of restaurant and other public prayer is to gain man's attention, rather than God's.

Barb and I didn't have our children memorize a mealtime prayer. They just observed what we did, and then with a little coaxing they tried it on their own. I remember they used to pray for the dogs, the windows, the dishes, Mommy and Daddy, "hope we don't get sick," the neighbor kids, their dolls and toys — everything but the food. At the end we would prompt them: "Remember the food." "Oh yes, and bless this food amen."

I just know God's eyes fill with tears when He listens to children pray. If you really want to know how to pray, listen to children. They can teach you much about being real. Give up all that stuff you've been tossing at God all these years. It's a wonder it doesn't make Him sick sometimes.

It's also exciting to hear a new Christian pray. A friend of mine came to know Christ recently, and a week later several of us were together with him — people who had loved him right where he was during his struggle to find God. That night I heard his first public prayer. "Hi God, this is Jim," he started out, and then went on to thank God for the people sitting in that room. His prayer was so real, so open, so honest! But it probably would have raised eyebrows at the Wednesday night prayer meeting, because he didn't use all the "correct" terms, the thee's and thou's.

Prayer doesn't have to be a bunch of giggles and tinsel either. Some of my most honest prayers have been when I was under terrible burdens of mind. I screamed out, asking God if He really knew what He was doing by allowing me to go through these situations. And yet I didn't turn into a pile of ashes either. I think He appreciates my honesty. He knows I love Him, even though I don't always understand what He is doing in my life.

Far too much of my prayer life has been spent doing what was expected rather than what was real. I don't like to feel a distance between God and myself when I pray. I get tired of all the guilt that has been heaped upon me in sermons and discussion about how, when, where, how long, and which words to pray.

Prayer is not a place, or style, or certain words, or King James English, or position of body. It is a natural outflow of feelings, requests, and thanksgiving from a child to his heavenly Father.

Of course, when I pray I'm not telling God anything He doesn't already know. He doesn't say, "Mercy me. I didn't know that."

For half a century I've been ripped off by folks laying their guilt trips on me about the beautiful world of prayer, and I just thank God for the people and books — and of course, the most important book, the Bible — for helping me begin my pilgrimage of prayer.

PART IX

HOW GOD GAVE US OUR DREAM HOUSE

33

THE MAKING OF A MIRACLE

PRAYER WAS INSTRUMENTAL in helping us find a new home — through a process we can look back on as a miracle.

Beginning the day Barb and I were married, I had a special dream house in mind. It was a Southern colonial, with pillars, weeping willows over the drive, a deck off the bedroom where I could pad around in my jammies, the privacy of acres of woods, and a front porch with a rocking chair, looking out onto a peaceful yard.

There was only one problem. Barb doesn't really like Southern colonial homes with pillars. And there is no way I could insist, because I've discovered that the home is the extension of the wife's personality, while the business is the extension of the husband's. I had to let Barb pick out our home—but I kept working on my list of wants in a house.

One of the reasons I wanted such a large home was to have room to entertain traveling missionaries, teachers, pastors, and friends. We had actually been doing this all along, squeezing them in among the family, which was not all that bad. But how nice it would be to give them a private room with a bath, and give them special treatment in an elegant setting!

The Bible shows us how Christians should take guests into their home, show them hospitality, and send them on their way with a gift:

> Dear friend, you are doing a good work for God in taking care of the traveling teachers and missionaries who are passing through. They have told the church here of your friendship and your loving deeds. I am glad when you send them on their way with a generous gift. For they are traveling for the Lord, and take neither food, clothing, shelter, nor money from those who are not Christians, even though they have preached to them. So we ourselves should take care of them in the Lord's work. (3 John 5-8)

Every once in a while, I brought up the subject to Barb, but she didn't seem too interested in moving to a larger home. We had a nice home and there was little motivation for her to leave, other than some minor conflicts with a lady next door with whom we shared a driveway.

Then a mean dog moved in behind our home. Every time we would let our perfect puppies out into the backyard, this dog would raise a fuss and begin fighting with them through the fence. I squirted him with the hose once in a while, but decided this was not a good way to maintain a Christian testimony with his masters, who never seemed to notice the dog's bad attitude.

On the other side of us, a fine family with seven boys moved out and some young, hippie-type people moved in and began playing their loud rock music. We would wake up at 3 A.M. with our bed vibrating to the bass notes. Cars raced up and down the street all night. There was an occasional loud fight outside our bedroom window, and we would find empty six-packs in the rose bushes the next morning.

I'm a little threatened by this type of people, but Barb

had the courage to approach them. They seemed apologetic, but the beat went on.

When I next brought up the subject of moving, Barb thought it might be something we should look into.

I had been talking with Dan Tradal, one of our Christian friends and a real estate salesman. From a tax and investment standpoint he thought we should find a bigger house. With Barb now agreeable to a move, I gave Dan the description of my dream house, just for fun. Several items on my list made him smile, but he wrote down all of them, including these:

- close to the central city (I don't like to commute.)
- grounds that wouldn't take too much work (On my pleasure scale, I put lawn work somewhere between having bamboo shoots pushed under my fingernails and being forced to walk on hot coals barefooted.)
- privacy
- room for my audio studio
- lots of storage room, because I collect things
- room for a tennis court
- a view of the mountains
- a place for a home office or den

To find all that in one house seemed an impossible deal. Dan called a couple of weeks later with a house for us to look at, and we went to see it. There was a guard at the gate, it had an acre of manicured garden, and inside it looked like the White House. It just wasn't us. Besides, having a guard at the gate would discourage people from dropping by for a visit. And since our son Tim was a mechanic and proud of his greasy clothes, the guard probably wouldn't let him in.

Two weeks later Dan called again. A house I had seen from the outside and liked was for sale. It was a white colonial on a large piece of ground, but quite run down, and a little further out of town than I really wanted. It did, however, have room for a tennis court. After seeing it, I said, "No, Lord, I don't think this is the home You want us to have." I began wondering if He just wanted us to stay where we were.

Then one day while driving, I was listening to Kay Arthur's tapes on prayer. She reminded me of this verse:

The reason you don't have what you want is that you don't ask God for it. (James 4:2)

Since I had never really been specific with God in prayer before, I thought I would practice. I prayed something like: "Lord, You know the dream house I have in mind. You know we want it to serve Your people. So I pray right now that You will give us the home even today. And, by the way, as You know, we're still missing that sound track, and I ask that You'll allow us to find it today." At the time I was doing missionary films, and the lab couldn't find one of the soundtracks that we needed to finish a film.

That evening the lab called and said they had found the missing sound track.

When I returned to my office, I found a note from Dan saying he had found a home he wanted us to look at. The time on Dan's note was before I had prayed, which brings to mind the Scripture that says, "Remember, your Father knows exactly what you need even before you ask him" (Matthew 6:8).

I called Dan. The price he quoted made me smile. It was well over what we could afford. However, we thought it would be fun to see a home in that price bracket, so we made an appointment. It was on a bluff overlooking Lake Washington and the mountains. We drove down a long tree-lined driveway, past a lighted tennis court (I had forgotten to ask for lights), past a swimming pool (I didn't even have a swimming pool on the list), and past a fountain, and stopped in front of a beautiful brick home surrounded by four acres of natural woods—right in the heart of the city! Right by the swimming pool was a separate little house with a living room, fireplace, kitchen, bathroom, dressing rooms, and storage rooms—an ideal place where guests could get together after a day of tennis and swimming to play guitars and sing, without disturbing the neighbors.

Inside the main house was the spiral staircase I had asked for, as well as a "dream kitchen" (according to Barb), with an upright barbecue and a breakfast nook with a spectacular view of water and mountains. The beautiful dining room had lots of windows, and there were also seven breathtaking bedrooms and six baths. Barb, in her practical way, was looking around for the garbage cans. I made the comment that people living in a house like this didn't have garbage.

I was ready to buy it after seeing the main floor, but Barb reminded me we had to have room for the audio studio. On the way to the basement, we passed an office which I could make my headquarters when at home, a storage area where we could keep extra food and Barb's canning supplies, and a huge storage area where the furnace and pool filter were located—plenty of room for my junk. By then my pulse was 120.

Downstairs we discovered a fully equipped film studio with rewinds, projection screen, and film storage—a perfect setup for our film activity. We walked through another door and came into a room that was the ideal size for an audio studio, even built out from the rest of the house so there would be no noise from footsteps up above—absolutely perfect in every way!

The upstairs had a place for Barb's art studio and sewing room. There was a study and a wood-paneled library-den with a fireplace (one of four in the house), and a bar we could use for milkshakes and pop.

The three-car garage would give me plenty of workshop room, and the greenhouse I forgot to ask for would give Barb room for her flowers. The treehouse for our guests' children was next to a set of swings in a beautiful little park-like area, which also included a covered sandbox. There was even room for horseshoe pits. The swimming pool had a bubble over it so we could swim year-round.

A wire fence enclosed most of the four acres—perfect to keep in our puppies and yet give them room to roam. There was also a double kennel with a dog run. (The Lord knew we had two dogs — so nothing strange about that.)

It was a nice dream. The Lord had shown us a home with everything on my list, and more. We believed it was the one He wanted us to have, and we prayed, "Lord, we can't afford that much. Please work a miracle if You want us to have this house."

We gave the house to the Lord, knowing it was His, but not knowing how He was going to provide money to pay for it. We felt strongly that if our giving and our ministries to friends and the church would be harmed in any way by buying a new house, we wanted to forget it! We would live in a tent if we had to choose between a new house and our ministries, even though the house was going to be used primarily for His service.

As we drove away, I stopped the car at the top of the little hill at the end of the lane, and Dan, Barb, and I prayed that the Lord would allow us to buy this home. We asked Him to help us confirm in our own minds the price He would have us pay for the home as well as the amount of the down payment. And wouldn't you know (when you're dealing with miracles), we all independently came up with identical figures. "Now, Lord," we asked, "how are You going to pay for your house? It's a lot of money."

A couple of weeks passed. The phone rang. A large company in Seattle asked me to consider taking their account, a client that had been the target of every advertising agency in town. For them to call me was a miracle in itself. And here I was being asked to take the account without ever meeting a single person at the company!

I found out later that one of our media friends had given us a good recommendation. He's a wonderful guy, but I doubt whether he fully understands how he was working for God in that project.

When Barb overheard my conversation with these people, she began dancing around the office. She knew this was the answer—the house was ours!

In effect, the Lord had agreed with us that we should not disturb our other ministries with a large house payment, so

He provided a new client to help pay the bills—just another routine miracle.

With the owner's agent, we began negotiations for the purchase. We still didn't feel we could pay the full price the owner wanted nor handle the large down payment, so we made an offer—the full price, but no interest. It wasn't surprising that the owner rejected it out of hand.

Following the rejection of our first offer, Barb, Dan, and I had lunch and discussed this "death of a vision." The Lord taught me that many times the Lord will allow things to "fall through" to help us grow spiritually as we lean on Him for guidance. I was ready to accept the seller's full price, knowing the Lord would provide the money through our new client, even though we felt the property was somewhat overpriced.

Barb felt we could do better on the terms. (We make a good team—she tempers my dreams with facts. And the facts were simply that we could not easily handle the full price the owner wanted for the house.)

We left our lunch with Dan without any further plans. Later that day I called Dan and suggested he present another offer—this time, the price the Lord had given us the first day we saw the house. I had a feeling our new offer would probably not be accepted either, so I put away in a "new home" file all the information I had been gathering about the house—including a list of missionaries, teachers, pastors, and lay workers we could invite to stay with us, a list of all the things to do to get ready to move, and a list of improvements and maintenance projects I wanted to do at the new house—adding a cover over the tennis court, putting in more security lighting, and cleaning out the greenhouse. Even if our counter offer was considered seriously, I thought a response would be weeks in coming.

We prayed for the seller, that his heart would soften and that he would be open to our terms. We were dealing only with his agent, and we were driving her nearly crazy.

After we made our second offer, she said she thought it would not be accepted and wanted us to make another offer.

Dan explained as best he could that the amount we were offering was all God wanted us to pay for the house, and we had to stay with that figure. I can imagine the frustrating conferences in that real estate office as they talked about the "weirdos" who were acting and talking as if the house were already theirs.

The day after I began filing away all the "new home" information, Dan called to say the seller was beginning to come down on his price.

I had been teaching a Bible study on Friday evenings, and many in the group had been praying we would get the dream house. Several had even gone to the property and were convinced this was the Lord's house for us. One of our friends even "claimed" the house for the Lord. I was concerned about how she would react if we didn't get it.

As we met again on a Friday evening, Barb was called from the group to the phone. She came back and announced that the Lord had given us the house, at the price He had given us that first day. Everyone cheered. Dan came over later in the evening to sign the contract.

Later, one of the women who attended the Friday study group was talking with people at a Bible bookstore called The Bridge, and was telling them about the miracle of our getting the home. They were thrilled, because their Bible study group had seen an article in the paper about the house, and had "claimed" it for the Lord.

The day after we moved in, nearly a hundred people attended a dedication service. (We invited the group from The Bridge to join us.)

Sometimes we don't have because we don't ask. I'm not saying everyone will get the home of his dreams just by asking for it. But if it will be used to honor God, and it is His will for you, consider it done. God is not through working miracles yet!

PART X

OTHER THAN THAT, I HAVE NO OPINION

34

AT
PEACE

WHILE SITTING IN MY CAR RECENTLY, I experienced the most overwhelming feeling of peace I have ever known.

Do you know what my next thought was? I wondered when I was going to get zapped by God, and have something go wrong!

How foolish that is — because God wants my best. The experience of peace He gave was the logical result of my wanting to serve Him with all my heart. He's not some cosmic monster sitting on the clouds and zapping people who are having fun or smiling too much. God wants me to have joy in my heart, to have peace, contentment, fulfillment, love.

One of the key principles in finding this peace with God is OBEDIENCE. When we obey God—when we walk in the center of His will with our focus in His Word, loving and serving other people—His peace is the natural result.

The second important thing for me is to give up control. I so much want things to happen on my time schedule, the way I want them to work out. When I give control of my life to God, I know I'm in the hands of Someone Who cared enough for me to die in my place. Someone who wants the best for me and wants to give me the desires of my heart. My tendency is to fit God into MY plans. What I try to live out is fitting me into HIS plans. It just works much better that way.

I love the story in John 9 about the blind man Christ healed. Afterward, when some of the religious men of the day were talking to the man and saying some awful things about Christ, he said something that still brings tears to my eyes: "All I know is that once I was blind, but now I can see."

Now I can see.... I echo his statement of wonder. Christ is real to me, and no one can do or say anything that would make Him any less real. I've proved His reality to my satisfaction, and that's something no one can argue with. He is giving me insights into why I should act differently than what my nature wants me to. I'm learning how to love as God wants me to love.

There's a plaque on my mother's wall saying, "Prayer changes things." I agree — and what has changed most is me. I really don't know how people without Christ face the day. I guess that's why so many of them jump off bridges or take drug overdoses. I probably would have done something like that too, if God, through Christ, hadn't reached down His hand to me.

I assume God has many more things for me to learn, more impurities to burn out of my life, more struggles for me to endure so I can be more valuable to others by sharing the comfort God gives me through each situation.

This has been the story of my pilgrimage in life so far. Thanks for traveling with me through this book. And thanks for giving me a little room to be different from you — to have different opinions — to approach Christianity and its institutions a little differently than you might. We are members of the same family, parts of the same body, and it takes all of us to make it work.

My hope is that before too long, Christ will return and

you and I can have fellowship face-to-face for eternity, and I won't need to talk to you by way of a book. What a happy thought!

With God's Love,
Chuck Snyder
P.O. Box 22696
Seattle, WA 98122